SOVIET POLICY TOWARDS
JEWS AND ISRAEL 1917-1974

SOVIET POLICY
TOWARDS
JEWS AND ISRAEL
1917-1974

by

LESTER SAMUEL ECKMAN

SHENGOLD PUBLISHERS, INC.
New York City

*To my wife Susan
and my children
Israel and Benjamin.*

ISBN 0-88400-005-2
Library of Congress Catalog Card Number: 73-93237
Copyright © 1974 by Lester Samuel Eckman
All rights reserved
Published by Shengold Publishers, Inc.
45 W. 45th St., New York, N.Y. 10036

Printed in the United States of America

CONTENTS

INTRODUCTION

This study proposes to trace the history of treatment of Jews in Russian society from the time of the Tsars until the present. To this end the author examines the cultural and religious life under the Tsars and compares it with the attrition of that life under the Soviet system beginning with the views of Karl Marx that influenced the creation of the Soviet system and tracing the changes that took place during the regimes of Lenin, Stalin, Khrushchev, and Brezhnev. One chapter will examine the ties between Communism and Zionism and a final chapter will explore Soviet Foreign Policy in the Middle East from 1948 to 1974.

One important thesis of the author is that although economic and political strictures were severe under the Tsars, Jews in the Pale of Settlement were nevertheless allowed to follow their religious and cultural preferences and Jewish culture flourished. Under the Soviet system, although anti-Semitism is officially disavowed, Jewish cultural life has been systematically expunged by Kremlin leaders.

❄   ❄   ❄   ❄   ❄

I wish to express my abiding gratitude to distinguished scholars and educators Professors Salo Baron and the late Henry Roberts of Columbia University and Professor Abraham Katsh, President of Dropsie University, whose guidance and direction have been a constant source of inspiration in the quest to expand the frontiers of knowledge of Eastern European Jewry.

I extend my gratitude to Professor Bernard Lander, President of Touro College, New York, for his constant support in my endeavors.

My thanks also go to my friends Joel Saibel and Linda Herwerth for their editorial assistance.

And finally, it gives me great pleasure to thank Mr. Moshe Sheinbaum, President of Shengold Publishers, and his staff for their unstinting efforts in the preparation of the manuscript for publication.

August, 1974   L. S. E.

CHAPTER ONE

JEWISH LIFE UNDER THE TSARS

In 1791 Russian Jews were ordered henceforth to make their homes within restricted districts established by the Tsarist regime —the "Pale of Jewish Settlement."

A later statute of 1835 "defined more definitively" the Pale of Settlement, which was to include the provinces of Vilna, Grodno, Volhynia, Minsk, Bessarabia, Podolia, Bialystok, Ekaterinoslav, Kiev (except the city of Kiev), Kherson (without Nikolaev), Moghilev and Vitebsk (without the villages), Tauride (without Sevastopol), Chernigov and Poltava (without the Cossack villages).

In April, 1843, all Jews living within a thirty-mile-wide strip along the frontier between Prussia and Austria were ordered to be transferred into the interior of the respective border countries. Those owning houses were permitted two years to sell them. Courland, Latvia, and the provinces of the kingdom of Poland, which were later annexed by Russia in 1863, were added to the Pale of Jewish Settlement. The boundaries set by the decree of 1835 remained more or less intact until 1917.[1]

Although Jews were restricted to these areas and were subject to discrimination in higher education and were heavily taxed, they at first enjoyed educational, religious, communal, and some economic autonomy within the Pale under Jewish communal organizations called *Kahals*. This autonomy was, however, abolished by the decree of December 19, 1844 which placed the transfer of Jews in the cities and towns under the jurisdiction of the central Russian Government. The decree ordered that all adminis-

---

[1]See Salo W. Baron, *The Russian Jew* (New York: Macmillan Co., 1964), pp. 20-21, 39, 55, 64.

trative duties of the *Kahals* be turned over to the police districts and that all functions of an economic and fiscal nature be transferred to the municipalities and town councils.[2]

In 1827, under Tsar Nicholas I (1825-1855), the "canton system" was established under which Jewish children were recruited for long years in military service to the Tsar. Russian recruits normally served in the Tsar's army for twenty-five years, beginning at the age of eighteen. Jewish children, however, were taken at the age of twelve and placed in a "preparatory establishment for military training." The cantonists were sent to remote places, and every effort was made to convert them to Christianity. Many of the Jewish recruits did not survive the rigorous discipline in the preparatory establishments for military training. Others saved themselves by embracing Russian Orthodoxy. Naturally, the Jews did everything within their power to keep their children from being conscripted into the Tsar's army. To frustrate their attempts at evasion, Nicholas ordered the leaders of each community to fill a quota of children, while informers and professional kidnappers added to the demoralization and terror within the Jewish community.[3]

Although this system was abolished by Tsar Alexander II (1855-1881) in 1856, the Conscription Law of 1874 soon followed. It demanded that every able-bodied twenty years old, regardless of social status, enter the military service. The normal term was six years of active service and nine years in the reserves. This law meant that young men studying in the Yeshivoth (higher Talmudical academies) would no longer be exempt from military service.[4]

Rule by Alexander II also brought about the May Laws of

---

[2]Simon M. Dubnow, *History of the Jews in Russia and Poland* (Philadelphia: The Jewish Publication Society of America, 1918), II, 59ff. See also, Baron, *The Russian Jew*, p. 125.

[3]See Dubnow, *History of the Jews in Russia and Poland* pp. 13-29 and Baron, *The Russian Jew*, pp. 35-38.

[4]One of the great spiritual leaders of the time, Rabbi Israel Meir Kagan, wrote widely of his concern that the conscription law threatened the very existence of the Yeshivoth and he feared that without Yeshiva students to assume leadership in the Jewish communities the historic foundations of traditional Jewish life could crumble. See Israel Meir Kagan, *Michtevei Hafets Hayyim*, edited by Ariah Leib Kagan (New York: Saphrograph Co., 1953), p. 18.

1882 which prohibited Jews from settling anew outside of the towns and villages. They suspended the "completion of instruments of purchase of real property and merchandise in the name of the Jews" outside of towns and villages. They restricted the Jews from transacting business on Sundays or on Christian holidays. As a result, Jews suffered new economic hardship even within the confines of the Pale of Settlement.[5]

Under Alexander III (1881-1894), the government not only continued to enforce the May Laws but added other prohibitions, among them a *numerus clausus* for secondary schools and universities, a quota for Jewish students established under the pretext that students of the Jewish community were "quick in joining the ranks of the revolutionary workers." In 1887 a quota of ten percent was set for schools within the Pale, five percent outside the Pale, and three percent in St. Petersburg and Moscow. Subsequently, these percentages were reduced to seven, three and two respectively.[6]

Stimulated by this repressive legislation, the first wave of Russian Jews embarked upon the mass emigration that would bring two million of them to the shores of America by the outbreak of World War One, and ideologies began to emerge within the Jewish intellectual community to deal with the threat posed by the unending and escalating repression.

From Germany, the *Haskalah,* an eighteenth century Jewish Enlightenment, found its way to Russia. One of the main purposes of the *Haskalah* had been to bring secular education, in particular the language of the land, to the Jewish masses. Its adherents, known as *Maskilim,* endeavored to attune the Jews of the ghetto to social, economic and cultural mores of the society around them.[7] By the beginning of the nineteenth century the *Maskilim* had succeeded in putting a sizeable portion of German Jewry well on the road of assimilation.

---

[5]Dubnow, *History of the Jews in Russia and Poland,* II, 316; and Baron, *The Russian Jew,* pp. 56, 57, 96, 261.

[6]Baron, *The Russian Jew,* p. 57.

[7]Salo W. Baron, *A Social and Religious History of the Jews* (New York: Columbia University Press, 1937), II, 213-224; and Dubnow, *History of the Jews in Russia and Poland,* II, 125-189.

Although attempts were made by some Russian Jews to follow the pattern set by the Germans, traditionally-oriented Jews were not happy with the results of the *Haskalah* movement in Germany and inveighed against all attempts to secularize Jewish life and disturb the traditional Jewish life. After the May Laws of 1882 it became clear that not even the *Haskalah* movement could mitigate the political, economic and educational strictures against the Jews—whether traditional Jews favored it or not.

Two opposing types of secular Jewish nationalism succeeded the *Haskalah* in Eastern Europe: the Palestine-oriented *Hoveve Zion,* which gave birth to the *Bilu* and then Herzlian Zionism; and Simon Dubnow's Diaspora Nationalism, which was espoused by the *Bund.*

The original *Hoveve Zion* (Lovers of Zion) movement was a group of scattered societies that had begun to emerge in the 1860s. These groups met at a conference in Kattowitz, Silesia in November 1884, organized a federation, and elected Leo Pinsker (1821-1891) as their president. Their aim was to restore Jewish national life by colonizing Palestine.[8]

Bilu takes its name from the Hebrew *Beth Ya'cob Lechu ve-Nelcha* ("House of Jacob, come let us go" Isaiah 2:5). The members of this group were the first actual pioneers to settle in Palestine after the pogroms of 1881. The group consisted largely of university students who were moved by the tragic events in Russia to search for meaning in life as workers of the soil in Palestine. Their aim was to encourage and strengthen immigration and colonization through the establishment of agricultural colonies, built on cooperative-social foundations. One of the first colonies founded by *Bilu* was Rishon le-Zion.[9]

Herzlian Zionism was the final outcome of this response to the growing persecution in Eastern Europe. Theodor Herzl (1860-1904), in Paris as a correspondent for the famous newspaper *Neue*

---

[8]Of the vast literature on the *Hoveve Zion,* the following may be mentioned: Nahum Sokolow, *History of Zionism 1600-1918,* with an introduction by A. J. Balfour (London, 1919), II, 281ff; S. L. Citron, *Toldot Hibbat Zion* (Odessa, 1914) Vol. I: B. Dinaburg, *Hibbat Zion* (Tel Aviv, 1932) Vol. I.

[9]See the Manifesto of the *Bilu* in Sokolow, *History of Zionism,* II, 332ff. See also Ismar Elbogen, *A Century of Jewish Life,* translated by Moses Hadas, (Philadelphia: The Jewish Publication Society of America, 1914), pp. 255ff, and 263.

Freie Presse, was aroused by the Dreyfus case. He struggled with the Jewish problem and arrived at the following conclusion: the Jewish people must have a Jewish state in Palestine; a charter for such a state should be obtained from Turkey; and a society must be launched to organize the mass emigration of Jews to Palestine.[10]

The second type of Jewish nationalism grew out of the interpretation of Jewish history made by the Russian Jewish historian Simon M. Dubnow. He claimed that the spiritual powers of the Jewish people and their unity were preserved by the organized Jewish community during the two thousand years of exile. He believe that the unity of the Jews did not depend upon a national territory, or even upon an independent state. Their unity was kept alive by communal organizations within whose framework Jewish culture and religion had continued their growth. The Jewish Socialist Party, organized in Russia in 1897 and known as the *Bund,* had a particularly strong influence among Jewish workers in such densely populated Jewish centers as Warsaw, Minsk, Vitebsk, and Bialystok. The Bund was a militant group which participated in the overthrow of the Tsarist government by organizing demonstrations and strikes. After the Russian Revolution of 1917 a part of the Bund joined the Jewish section of the Communist Party, while those who did not were persecuted by the Soviets. In Poland, the Bund established schools, conducted cultural works in the Yiddish language, and formed youth groups and workers' cooperatives. It opposed Zionism and was antagonistic to Hebrew as the Jewish national tongue. The aim of the Bund was to develop political and socialistic consciousness within the masses of Jews and to emphasize equality.[11]

---

[10]Sources of immense value on Theodor Herzl and his work are his *Tagebucher,* edited by Leon Kellner (Berlin, 1922-23), 3 Vols., and his *Gesammelte Zionistische Werke* (Berlin, 1934), 5 Vols. See also his *A Jewish State,* translated by S. d'Avigdor, 2nd revision with a foreword by Israel Cohen (London, 1934).

[11]See Dubnow, *History of the Jews in Russia and Poland,* II, 55-58, 132-142; and S. M. Dubnow, *Nationalism and History: Essays on Old and New Judaism,* edited with an introduction by Koppel S. Pinson (Philadelphia: The Jewish Publication Society of America, 1918); see also Koppel S. Pinson, "Arkady Kremer, Vladimir Medem and the Ideology of the Jewish Bund," in *Jewish Social Studies,* VII (1945), 234-64; and Jacob Sholem Hertz, *Doires Bundisten* (New York, 1965); and Baron, *The Russian Jew,* pp. 168-172, 205, 224.

One index of the differences between these two ideologies was their preferences for a Jewish national language. Zionism fostered the regeneration of Hebrew as the national language while Diaspora Nationalism and the Bund favored Yiddish, the vernacular spoken by German and Russian Jews. Although Hebrew was not spoken among Jews until these attempts at regeneration by Zionism in the nineteenth century, it had continued as the language of prayer and literature. In the 1880's Eliezer ben Yehuda insisted that the Jewish people must regain their homeland together with their national language. His pioneering in the revival of Hebrew as a spoken language was taken up enthusiastically by many followers.[12] Yiddish began to develop when Jews from France settled along the Rhine, and their vocabulary was augmented by many words from various medieval German dialects of their new neighbors. Expulsions and persecutions forced the Jews to move from place to place, increasing the difference between their speech and that of the surrounding populace. When the German Jews migrated to Bohemia, Poland and Lithuania, they took with them their medieval German dialect, at the same time adopting more Hebrew and Slavic words. As ghetto life became the norm, the Jew in the ghetto was cut off from the cultural life of the surrounding area. This isolation, added to the special Jewish way of life, was also a factor in the development of Yiddish. As the Jews continued moving eastward, Ukranian, White Russian and Russian elements entered the Yiddish language. When Yiddish-speaking immigrants moved westward to the New World, the vocabulary of Yiddish expanded to include English terms and Spanish words in Argentina. These diversified additions have by now greatly enhanced the Yiddish language.

There were other diametrically opposed differences between the Zionism of Herzl and his followers and the Diaspora Nationalism of Dubnow and the Bund as they vied for supremacy in Eastern European Jewish life. But they also shared one likeness: they both represented revolutionary departures from the traditionally-oriented Jews who are now known as Orthodox, and who

---

[12]Sokolow, *History of Zionism*, I, 287; II, 284, 384. See also the biography of Yehuda at the introduction to the tenth volume of his dictionary.

espouse strict adherence to the traditional teachings of Judaism.[13] The Jewish masses, who closely followed the ideological struggle between these three groups, were constantly wooed for support by the leaders of each.

In the first decades of the twentieth century Russian Jewry was engulfed by a series of bestial pogroms. Major massacres took place at Kishinev in 1903, at Bialystok in 1905, and in other Russian cities and towns in the following years. The first pogrom at Kishinev was instigated by P.A. Krushevan, editor of the conservative newspaper, *Bessarbets,* which was heavily subsidized by the Tsarist government. In two days (April 6-7) of killing and plundering, forty-five Jews were killed, eighty-six were seriously injured, and five hundred were less seriously wounded. During the pogrom, one thousand five hundred houses and shops were looted or destroyed.[14] Bialystok was one of the 660 Jewish communities which subsequently suffered from the wave of plundering and killing. In a span of one week (October 19-25) in 1905 the Jews of Russia suffered about one thousand dead, seven to eight thousand wounded, and property losses of a hundred and thirty-one million dollars.[15]

These massacres triggered the next wave of mass emigration from Russia and spurred the formation of the first Jewish self-defense body in Russia.[16] During the First World War the misery of Russian Jews intensified and continued unabated after the war, particularly during the period of violence that accompanied the Bolshevik Revolution when Jewish religious and communal life was severely disrupted.[17]

Following the First World War both the political Zionism of

[13]Baron, *The Russian Jew,* pp. 158-181; Dubnow, *History of the Jews in Russia and Poland,* III, 40-65.

[14]Baron, *The Russian Jew,* p. 69; and *American Jewish Year Book* (1903-1904), V, 19-22, 39, 109, 111-112, 129-130, 133-141.

[15]Baron, *The Russian Jew,* p. 69; *American Jewish Year Book* (1906-1907), VIII, 36, 37, 79-89.

[16]Baron, *The Russian Jew,* p. 69; Dubnow, *History of the Jews in Russia and Poland,* III, 80, 87ff, 96, 116ff, 120, 129, 150. See also Louis Greenberg, *The Jews in Russia* (New Haven: Yale University Press, 1944), pp. 52, 64, 81, 155, 158.

[17]Rabbi Israel Meir Kagan first requested financial aid from Western Jews for the refugees of the First World War and for victims of the Bolshevik Revolution. See *Michtevei Hafets Hayyim,* II, 1-7, 60-61.

Herzl and his followers and the Diaspora Nationalism of Dubnow were accorded recognition by the Western World. The Balfour Declaration states:

> His Majesty's Government views with favour the estab-
> lishment in Palestine of a national home for the Jewish
> people, and will use their best endeavours to facilitate
> the achievement of this object, it being clearly under-
> stood that nothing shall be done which may prejudice
> the civil and religious rights of existing non-Jewish com-
> munities in Palestine, or the rights and political status
> enjoyed by Jews in any other country.[18]

In the Versailles Treaty of 1919 Dubnow's principles of cultural nationalism were recognized in the treaty's insistence on
the right of national self-determination. In the case of the Jews,
the new states created by the treaty were obligated to protect
the cultural, religious, and linguistic autonomy of the Jewish
minority who differ from the majority in race, language or religion. Jewish cultural rights were later granted to Polish, Lithuanian, Estonian and Latvian Jewish communities. In Poland, the
government was obligated to assure the Jews instruction in their
own language and to provide the proportional share of public
funds allocated to Jewish schools. Jews could not be forced to
violate the Sabbath.

And so it came about that as Poland achieved its independence from Russia, Russian Jewry was divided into two camps—
the one in Poland enjoying, at least in theory, varying degrees
of religious, educational, and communal freedom; and the one
in Russia subjected to the most extreme oppression and persecution and the systematic destruction of their traditional way of
life.

Though Jews had suffered political, economic, social and educational discrimination under the Russian Tsars, they were none-
theless permitted, within the Pale of the Jewish Settlement, to

---

[18]*American Jewish Year Book* (1919-1920), p. 659; Elbogen, *A Century of Jewish Life*, p. 478.

practice their religion and engage in creative literary activity in Hebrew and Yiddish and the resulting religious and cultural movements (to be discussed in Chapter Two) stand as evidence of a golden age of Jewish cultural creativity. With the advent of the Soviet regime, although the Jews do not officially suffer from political, social, economic, or educational discrimination to the extent they did under the Tsars, Jewish religion and Hebrew culture have been systematically destroyed by the Kremlin authorities. This will become clearer in subsequent chapters dealing with Soviet policies toward the Jews from Lenin through the Brezhnev regime.

CHAPTER TWO

JEWISH RELIGIOUS AND CULTURAL LIFE
UNDER THE TSARS

The Jews of Tsarist Russia were the spiritual progenitors of many diverse philosophies and movements that continue to have a profound impact upon Jewish life today. This brief depiction of some of the major movements of that time will provide a background for subsequent chapters which hope to show the ways in which Judaism has been impoverished by Soviet Russia.

Traditional Talmudic culture produced a long chain of renowned and pietistic rabbis, scholars and protagonists of the rabbinic tradition. One of the earliest and most renowned figures in the Talmudic tradition was Rabbi Eliyahu (1720-1797) of Vilna. Rabbi Eliyahu was born in Vilna, and as a result of the great respect that Ashkenazic[1] Jews accorded him, he became known as the Gaon ("genius") of Vilna and his name became a household word representing the highest standards of Talmudic learning and devotion. He held no official community position, but spent most hours of the day and night engrossed in his studies, with one or two hours a day of teaching for a small number of brilliant students.

> As he aged, the Gaon of Vilna intensified his studies. . . . in accord with his self-imposed regimen, he committed to memory the Talmudim and cognate rabbinic literature, as well as all the Scriptures, along with their vast exegesis.

---

[1]The name "Ashkenazic" was applied to Jews of Germany and Northern France from the tenth century on. In the middle of the sixteenth century the term "Ashkenazic" came to include the Jews of Eastern Europe.

> ... Convinced that ignorance of secular learning was a
> hindrance to a proper understanding of Torah, Eliyahu
> included secular matters in his program; he studied phi-
> losophy, history, astronomy, mathematics and anat-
> omy . . .[2]

It was pupils of the Gaon of Vilna who were to found the two
great Russian *yeshivot*—Volozhin and Mir, thereby providing Russian Jews with a thoroughly educated rabbinical elite for more
than a century.

Rabbi Israel Baal Shem Tov (1700-1760) spoke to a very different need than did the intellectual rabbinical tradition. The
dialectical, intellectual method of the rabbis often failed to move
the masses of working Jews who were most afflicted by the growing loss of autonomy in the Pale of Settlement. The arrogant de-
meanor of the rich and learned Jews engendered pain and despair
among the poorer Jews and they began to rebel against the rabbinical authority within their communities.

Rabbi Israel Baal Shem Tov was of the people and walked
freely among them. His Hasidic Judaism, a contribution in the
sphere of intimate religious emotional life, taught that the humblest of men could find God since his being was diffused throughout all of creation and since the Creator seeks many forms of
service from many different kinds of men. Since sadness is a
hindrance to devotion, all worship must be joyful and in a spirit
of enthusiasm. Devotion itself is what creates spiritual value.

The Hasidic movement—with its innate protest against a lack
of democracy, against the dry dialectical intellectualism of the
rabbis, and against the emotionless observance of religious obliga-
tions—brought into the most despairing lives a consciousness of
spiritual power and a joyous sense of immersion in an all pervasive, ever-present Creator and thereby opened a door long closed
to the poor and suffering Jew. It offered a new type of leader who,
after difficult struggles with more traditional Jews, reached an
uneasy compromise that allowed Hasidism to remain a powerful

---

[2]M. M. Yosher, "Eliyahu of Vilna," in *Jewish Leaders*, edited by Leo Jung,
(Jerusalem, 1954), p. 31.

force in much of Russia—in the Ukraine, Podolia, Volhynia, and Russian Poland.[3]

Jews under Tsarist Russia were also responsible for the Musar (Moral) movement. The historical setting for the birth of the Musar movement was amidst the uncompromising attitude of the rabbinical authorities, the stagnation of Hasidism, the attempts by the followers of the *Haskalah* to undermine Hasidism as well as traditional Judaism, and the impenetrable wall that separated the Jewish population from the Russian people.

The founder of the Musar movement was Rabbi Israel Salanter (1810-1883). When he began his work, nineteenth-century Lithuanian Jewry was in the throes of a profound religious upheaval and spiritual well-springs of Jewish life were threatening to run dry. The aggressive *Haskalah* movement aimed at reshaping traditional Jewish life in the spirit of the modern enlightenment, but its growth was largely due to a fatal weakness which had grown up within the life of traditional Jewry itself—an unthinking observance of Torah law, observance that was a matter of habit and convention without sufficient regard for the spiritual content of the law. While there were of course some Jews dedicated to the study of ethical works, unthinking observance represented a growing difficulty for the Jewish community.

Rabbi Salanter addressed himself to this problem in pointing out that the spirit of the law was being neglected.

> We witness that an individual refrains from committing many sins, even at a time when he is forced to transgress a precept by a circumstance. There are more serious transgressions than these that a person will be lax in abstaining from committing them. An example is: a large proportion of our brethren will not eat without washing the hands. . . . However, in the case of slander, a grave sin, they will trespass easily. . . . Even the learned

---

[3]For details on the life and works of Rabbi Israel Baal Shem Tov, his disciples and the Hasidic movement see S. Dubnow, *Toledoth ha-Hassiduth* (Tel Aviv, 1931); D. Kahane, *Toledoth ha-Mekubalim, ha-Shebethaim ve-Hassidim*, 2 vols., (Tel Aviv, 1926); S. A. Horodetzky, *Ha-Hassiduth ve-Hassidim*, 4 vols., (Berlin, 1923); *Tanya*, Habad World Organization (Tel Aviv); Sheour Zalman, *Sefer Hassiduth* (Tel Aviv, 1947).

and almost God-fearing, too, are lax in keeping the moral precepts of the Torah, which, when they are transgressed, the Day of Atonement and also death will not expiate them.[4]

The Musar movement began to assume the responsibility for raising the standards of learning and morality in observing the laws of the Torah. It called for a spiritual and moral renaissance, a revitalization of the soul, an uprooting of distorted values, and the re-directing of the path of life. It stressed the perfection of the Torah, the necessity of perfection of deeds, and for a wholeness of the person who would be well-adjusted to God and to his fellowmen.[5] The movement had a major impact on Eastern European Jewry because its participants were not only witnesses but also active contributors to the historical events of their time. The multi-faceted movement was concerned with a laxity of morality within the Jewish community, the conditions of Jewish soldiers in the Tsarist army, the rise of the *Haskalah* among Jews, and Zionism. It also concerned itself with the economic, social, and political discrimination in Tsarist Russia, the problems of immigration, the religious and communal problems of Soviet Jews, and with the establishment of educational and rabbinical institutions. We have already seen, in Chapter One, that the *Haskalah* movement, the Jewish enlightenment of the eighteenth century, became a powerful force in Russian Jewish life, springing from a dissatisfaction with traditional Judaism and from a sense that a new era was upon the Jews—one that demanded new solutions. The city of Vilna[6] was the center of the *Haskalah* and the home of such prominent writers as Mordecai Aaron Ginsberg (1796-1846) and the poet Abraham Baer Lebensohn (1794-1878).[7] Religious followers of the *Haskalah* strove to achieve a synthesis

---

[4]Rabbi Israel Salanter, "Igeret ha-Musar," in *Or Israel*, edited by Rabbi Isaac Blazer (Vilna, 1900), pp. 106ff.

[5]Dov Katz, *Tenuath ha-Musar* (Tel Aviv, 1952), I, 60-64.

[6]For more information on the city of Vilna at this time, see S. J. Fuenn, *Kiryah Nemana*.

[7]On the life and works of Mordecai Ginsburg and Abraham Lebensohn, see Joseph Klausner, *Historia Sel ha-Sifruth ha-Ivrith ha-Hadasah* (Jerusalm, 1954), I, 270-287, 287-305.

of Judaism with the modern world by combining religious learning and secular knowledge. The writers who followed this movement produced a flowering of Yiddish and Hebrew literature in prose and poetry to which we remain indebted today.

The *Haskalah* also produced, as we have seen in Chapter One, the nationalist and socialist movements. Of course, diverse branches of the nationalist movement were to fight each other bitterly, but they found harmony in one basic tenet: that the Jews had a natural right to live the life of a national minority, to choose for themselves how to express their Judaism or their Jewishness and to convey their national culture and tradition not only as individuals, as in the West, but also as a national group.

Much of the foundation of what is now the State of Israel was laid down by Jews of Tsarist Russia. Socialism and the communal life-style of the kibbutz, the idea of self-defense which grew into the formation of the *Haganah,* and A. D. Gordon's plan for a moral rebirth of Jewry through labor—stemming from Leo Tolstoy's ideas on the dignity of labor—are all cornerstones of Israeli life that were laid down by Russian Jews. Other Russian Jews who were instrumental in shaping the spiritual growth of Israel were Rabbis Abraham Kook, Nathan Zvi Finkel, and Mordecai Epstein.

These vital religious and cultural movements flourished in Tsarist Russia despite, or perhaps partly because of, hardships of discrimination and isolation. They were later to be systematically destroyed by the Soviet government in an atmosphere of active persecution and widespread assimilation, as we shall see in subsequent chapters.

Chapter Three

KARL MARX AND THE JEWS

With Karl Marx (1818-1883), the "Red Prussian," socialism sprang forth into revolutionary Communism. Where early socialists had forecast a gradual and peaceful evolution toward Utopia, Karl Marx advocated a sudden and violent proletarian revolution. Where his predecessors had mistrusted governments, Marx advocated a seizure of power by the working class and utilization of the instruments of government for securing proletarian welfare. Of all the socialist thinkers, Marx was the most dogmatic and the most confident. He was convinced that he alone possessed a knowledge of what the future of mankind would be and that that future would follow the strict laws which he had observed to govern human history.

Marx's Life

Though Marx was born and died in the nineteenth century, in spirit he belonged partly to the eighteenth century. He had been born a Jew of a rabbinical family but his father, Heschel Marx, had converted to Christianity in 1816 in order to practice law in Prussia. Like many converts, Marx struggled all his life with his Jewishness and often attacked Judaism bitterly.

Trained by his father in the rationalism of the Enlightenment, Marx early in life acquired the kind of faith in natural law that had characterized the thinkers of the Enlightenment; in his case it was faith in the natural laws of economic determinism and class struggle. From this followed his and his disciples' boast that their socialism alone was "scientific" as opposed to the "dreamy and unrealistic" doctrines of the utopian socialists.

As a student at the University of Berlin from 1836-1840, Marx came under the influence of Hegel's philosophy. He applied the

Hegelian dialectic to the class struggle which he had observed in the economic sphere. His "thesis" was the bourgeoisie, his "antithesis" was the proletariat, and his "synthesis" was to be "a classless utopia issuing from the Communist revolution."

At the age of 30 Marx had finished the outlines of his theory of scientific revolutionary socialism. He had also been banished permanently from his native Germany because his atheistic articles had turned the authorities against him. In 1843 he was ordered to Paris and in 1845 he was exiled to Brussels by the government of Louis Phillippe, who feared his anti-bourgeois propaganda. Marx continued to read economics and discuss his theories with socialist and radical thinkers of his generation. He also began his long friendship and collaboration with Friedrich Engels (1820-1895). In many ways the two men made a striking contrast. Marx was poor and quarrelsome, a man of few friends. Except for his devotion to his wife and children, he was engrossed in his economic studies. Engels, on the other hand, was the son of a well-to-do German manufacturer and represented the family textile business in Liverpool and Manchester. He loved women, sports and high living in general. But he also hated the iniquities of industrialism. Both Marx and Engels became involved in the Communist League, a small international organization of radical workingmen. In 1847, the London office of the Communist League requested them to draw up a program. Engels wrote the first draft which Marx revised completely. The result, published in January, 1848, was the Manifesto of the Communist Party.

From 1849 until his death in 1883 Marx lived in London. There, partly because of his own financial mismanagement, Marx and his family experienced at first hand the misery of a proletarian existence in the slums of Soho. Poverty and near-starvation caused the death of three of his children. Eventually, he obtained a modest income through the generosity of Engels and from his own writings.

Marx wrote and studied constantly. He produced a series of pamphlets of which the most famous was *The Eighteenth Brumaire of Louis Napoleon,* a study of the fall of the short-lived Second French Republic. Throughout the 1850's he contributed a weekly article on British politics or international affairs to Horace Greeley's radical paper, *The New York Tribune*. He spent his days in the British Museum reading the reports of parliamentary investigating committees and piling up evidence of the working conditions of factory hands and miners, accumulating the material for his full-dress economic study, *Das Kapital*. The first volume of this massive analysis of capitalism appeared in 1867. Two further volumes, pieced together from his voluminous notes, were published after his death.

In 1864, Marx joined in the formation of the First International Workingmen's Association. The association was an ambitious attempt to organize workers of every country and every shade of radical belief. It soon began to disintegrate, however, and expired in 1876. Increasing persecution by hostile governments helped to bring about its demise but so, too, did the internal quarrels that repeatedly engaged its leaders and the rank and file of membership. Marx's own intolerance seems to have set an example that caused many of these difficulties.

The Communist Manifesto

Marx found three laws in the pattern of history: economic determinism, the existence of a class struggle with a dialectical nature, and the inevitability of communism. He believed that the nature of all areas of human life—society and government, religion, and art—was ultimately determined by economic conditions; that history is a process of struggle between the "haves" and the "have nots"; and that the class struggle was leading inevitably to a cataclysmic upheaval that would see the proletariat (the "have nots") victorious over the bourgeoisie (the "haves").

Today, more than a century after its original publication, the *Communist Manifesto* remains the classic statement of Marxian socialism. It opens with the dramatic announcement that "a spectre is haunting Europe—the spectre of Communism." It closes with a supremely confident appeal: "Let the ruling classes tremble of a Communist revolution. The proletarian have nothing to lose but their chains. They have a world to win. Workingmen of all countries unite."

Capitalism

Marx saw the capitalistic order as unjust and decaying and doomed to failure. Using Adam Smith's labor theory of value,[1] he advocated that only the worker should receive the profits from the sale of a commodity, since the value of the commodity should be determined by the labor of the man who produces it. He predicted that economic crises were bound to occur again and again under a system under which labor consumed too little and capital produced too much.

Modern industry, Marx contended, is a Frankenstein monster that will inevitably destroy the bourgeois society that now profits from it. It creates a mounting social pressure by narrowing the circle of capitalists to fewer and fewer individuals and by forcing more and more people down to the property-less status of proletarians. These pressures will increase to the point where a revolutionary explosion occurs. Landed property will be abolished outright; other forms of property will be liquidated more gradually through the imposition of severe taxes and denial of the right to inheritance. Eventually, social classes and tensions will vanish and we shall have an association in which "the free development of each is the condition for the free development of all."

Nationalism

Perhaps Marx's greatest error was in failing to observe the growing strength of nationalism. The Manifesto expected the class struggle to transcend national boundaries. In social and economic warfare, nation would not be pitted against nation, nor state against state; the proletariat would fight the bourgeoisie everywhere. In Marx's own lifetime, however, national differences and antagonisms were intensifying rapidly from day to day. Within a few months of the publication of the Manifesto, the Revolutions of 1848 revealed the antagonism between Italians and Austrians, Austrians and Hungarians, Hungarians and Slavs, Slavs and Germans. Nationalism awakened not only the bour-

---

[1]Adam Smith, *Selections from the Wealth of Nations* (Chicago: Henry Regenery, N.D.).

geoisie but also the laborers themselves who responded with increasing fervor to its powerful emotional appeal.

Religion

Marx saw religion as teaching working people to be patient all their lives and as comforting them with the hope of reward in a life to come, in heaven. As for those who live upon the labor of others, religion advocates that they be charitable, "thus providing a cheap justification for their whole exploiting existence and selling them, at a reasonable price, tickets to heavenly bliss." Marx held that religion is the "opiate of the masses," a kind of spiritual intoxicant for those who toil in poverty and long for some sort of decent human existence.

The Jews

It is interesting to note at the outset that most of Marx's original anti-Semitic statements in his correspondence and other writings have been eliminated in later editions by his various editors.

In addressing himself to the role of Jews in the process of emancipation of the masses of men from capitalism, Marx began by disagreeing with Dr. Bruno Bauer, a contemporary theologian and social philosopher. Bauer seems to have viewed the problem as a purely religious one—if the Jew is non-religious, he will be in the same position as the Christian, that is one step away from emancipation. Obstacles to the emancipation of the Jew exist only when he is religious and, therefore, alienated from the fundamental principles of Christianity. Marx asks us, however, to

> Look at the real Jew of our time: not the Jew of the Sabbath, whom Bauer considers, but the Jew of everyday life. What is the Jew's basis in our world? Material necessity, private advantage. What is the purpose of Jew's worship in this world? Usury. What is his worldly God? Money.[2]

---

[2]Karl Marx, "Die Fahigkeit der heutigen Juden und Christen frei zu werden," in *The Collected Works of Karl Marx and Friedrich Engels, 1841-1850*, Vol. I, March 1841-March, 1844. Edited by Franz Mehring, Stuttgart: Dietz Nachf, 1902, p. 425.

For Marx, the question of Jewish capacity for emancipation becomes "the question of which element in society must be overcome in order to abolish Judaism." The Jews' incapacity for emancipation depends on their relation to the whole enslaved world, and the difficulty of disengaging him from the practice of usury and the making of money. Marx held that Judaism contains an anti-social element which has achieved its present-day strength through a historical development in which the Jews eagerly collaborated. The essential goals of Judaism are practical needs, and egotism. The God of Israel is money. The bill of exchange is the real God of the Jew. Even the relations between the sexes have become an economic matter: "The woman is auctioned off."[3] Thus, Marx concluded, Jewish emancipation means, ultimately, "the emancipation of society from Judaism."[4]

The Jew has already freed himself in some way. He who is, for example, merely tolerated socially in Vienna plays an important role in determining the destiny of the entire German Empire through his economic power. The Jews have emancipated themselves to the extent that Christians have become Jews.[5] Judaism has maintained itself alongside of Christianity because its materialistic spirit has assured its viability in Christian society where it has achieved the most profound pinnacle of self-expression. The Jew who is a special member of bourgeois society remains only a special phenomenon of Judaism within that society. "Bourgeois society continuously brings forth the Jew from its entrails."

Marx's Assets and Shortcomings

Marx's Communist Manifesto is one of history's most influential works. It foreshadowed the remarkable character of present-day Communist propaganda—the constant sneering at bourgeois morality, bourgeois law, bourgeois property and the drama-filled reference to the "spectre haunting Europe" and to the proletarians who "have nothing to lose but their chains." The Manifesto anticipated the emphasis later to be placed on the party's

---

[3]*Ibid.*, pp. 428-29.
[4]*Ibid.*, p. 426.
[5]*Ibid.*, p. 430.

role in forging the working class revolution. The Communists, Marx declared in 1848, were a spearhead, "the most advanced section of the working class parties of every country," and the Communist Party had the advantage of clearly understanding the conditions and the ultimate results of the proletarian movement. The Manifesto also presaged the equally great role to be played by the state in the revolution. Among the policies advocated by Marx were centralization of credit in the hands of the state and extension of factories and instruments of production owned by the state. The Manifesto thus faintly but unmistakeably fore-shadowed the totalitarian state of the Soviet Union. Finally, it clearly established the line dividing Communism from other forms of socialism. Marx's dogmatism, his philosophy of history, and his belief in the inevitability of a total revolution—sweeping and violent—made his brand of socialism a thing apart. Like an omniscient religious prophet, Marx granted loyal legions of fol-lowers a full revelation of the universe and its meaning. He con-fidently expected his socio-economic gospel to supplant all others.

Certainly there are shortcomings in Marx's views. He over-simplified the complexities of human nature by neglecting the non-material interests and motives of men. The history of the century since the publication of the Communist Manifesto has demonstrated conclusively that neither proletarians nor bour-geoisie have fulfilled the simple stereotyped roles that Marx had envisioned. Labor has often behaved in unmarxian fashion by assuming a bourgeois outlook and mentality. Capitalism has put its own house in better order by eliminating the most glaring in-justices of the factory system.

As has been noted above, Marx's greatest error was his fail-ure to observe the growing strength of nationalism. In his own lifetime, national differences and antagonisms were increasing from day to day.

Whatever Marx's motives may have been in remaining as nar-rowminded and blind and, in some cases, it would seem intellec-tually dishonest about Jews, it seems clear and unfortunate that his anti-Semitism was so thorough-going and bitter and that in this area his otherwise meticulous scholarliness seems to have failed him. Marx's impact on the Soviet leaders and their ideologies since the Bolshevik Revolution is common knowledge. What is not so well known is that he left a legacy of anti-Semitism for the Bolshevik leaders and the Russian people to study and possibly apply. How much of it was and is being practiced by the Communist leaders in power and by the Russian people will be discussed in subsequent chapters.

Chapter Four

LENIN AND THE JEWS

In 1905 Lenin wrote "our propaganda includes the propaganda of atheism."[1] But this did not bring him to share Marx's anti-Semitic statements. For both philosophical and pragmatic reasons, Lenin was an implacable foe of anti-Semitism throughout his political career. Ideologically he postulated that anti-Semitism was contrary to the fundamental socialist tenet of equality. Pragmatically, he believed Jewish assimilation might have occurred much more rapidly had it not been for overt manifestations of anti-Semitism. In this all-pervading Jew-hatred Lenin sensed a fundamental danger to the Bolshevik Revolution,

> especially since the early disproportionate share of Jewish leadership in the Communist party was being used to excellent advantage by the anti-Soviet propagandists in and outside the country.[2]

On July 27, 1918, the Council of People's Commissars issued harsh decrees against any form of anti-Semitic propaganda.

> The Council of People's Commissars declares that the anti-Semitic movement and pogroms against the Jews are fatal to the interests of the workers' and peasants' revolution and calls upon the toiling people of Socialist Russia to fight this evil with all the means at their disposal.

---

[1]Vladimir Lenin, "Socialism and Religion," *Selected Works* (New York, n.d.), XI, 658.
[2]Salo Baron, *The Russian Jew*, p. 214.

29

National hostility weakens the ranks of our revolutionaries, disrupts the united front of the toilers without distinctions of nationality and helps only our enemies.

The Council of People's Commissars instructs all
Soviet deputies to take uncompromising measures to tear
the anti-Semitic movement out by the roots. Pogromists
and pogrom-agitators are to be placed outside the law.[3]

Although the last part was vague, it seems that while Sverd-
lov, a Jew, had written the main part of the declaration Lenin
himself had added the last paragraph.[4]

Lenin regarded the danger of anti-Semitism so seriously
that on March 31, 1919, he broadcast an appeal to the Russian
people to curb the anti-Semitic menace.[5]

Lenin and Zionism

Ironically, it was the Jewish communists who were instrumental in persuading Lenin and his regime to outlaw all Jewish
political parties, especially the Zionist organizations. During the
regime of Nicholas II, the Zionist movement "had become the
most potent force in Jewish public life despite the necessity of
long operating underground."[6] By 1918, when the Zionist movement was able to operate openly, it had 1,200 local Zionist groups
with some 300,000 members.[7] But in June, 1918, the Second Conference of the Jewish Communist Sections in Moscow adopted
the following resolution:

The Zionist party plays a counterrevolutionary role. It is
responsible for strengthening, among the backward Jewish masses, the influence of clericalism and nationalist
attitudes. In this way the class self-determination of the
Jewish toiling masses is undermined and the penetration

---

[3]*Ibid.*, p. 215. See also *Izvestia*, July 27, 1918.
[4]*Ibid.*
[5]Vladimir Lenin, *Sochinoniia*, 2nd ed., XXI (1932), 203. See also Anatolii
V. Lunacharskii, *Ob Antisemitizme* (Moscow, 1929).
[6]Baron, *The Russian Jew*, p. 208.
[7]*Ibid.*

of Communist ideas in their midst seriously hindered. Owing to its Palestine policy, the Zionist Party serves as an instrument of united imperialism which combats the proletarian revolution. In consideration of all these circumstances, the conference requests the Central Bureau to propose to pertinent authorities the promulgation of a decree suspending all activities of the Zionist Party in the economic, political, and cultural spheres. The communal organs, which are the mainstay of all reactionary forces within the Jewish people, must be suppressed.[8]

The Zionist movement was outlawed and 3,000 of its foremost leaders were arrested, many of whom were deported to Siberia's political labor camps.[9] Lenin's government also abolished the smaller groups of Labor Zionists, young Zionists, the People's Party (Folkisten), and the Bund. In a manner typical of totalitarian governments, political dissent was summarily silenced.

Lenin's Stand on Jewish Institutions

Because of the role the leaders of the Jewish Commissariat had assumed in abolishing the Jewish parties, the government found it difficult to appoint men of stature to these posts. Two leaders of the Jewish Commissariat, who were destined to preside over the dismantling of the organized Jewish community in Russia, were Samuel Agurskii and Simeon Dimanshtain (appointed Jewish Commissar by the Soviet Government in 1918). Soon after Dimanshtain assumed leadership, the Jewish Commissariat passed a resolution (October 20) suspending the operation of all Jewish institutions within the Jewish quarter. The Commissariat leaders argued that since the Jewish establishment was detrimental to the interest of the Jewish masses it was no longer worthy of a place in Jewish life.

Lenin's government instantly adopted the resolution and immediately began to dismantle all existing Jewish institutions. In

---

[8]*Ibid.*
[9]See L. Zenziper, *Eser Shnot Redifot* (Tel Aviv, 1930) for the story of the persecution of the Zionist movement in the Soviet Union.

June, 1919, Jewish establishments were outlawed by a Soviet government decree bearing the signatures of Agurskii and a rising young party official named Josef Stalin. Under the terms of the decree all synagogues were closed and their possessions expropriated. All youngsters under eighteen were prohibited from receiving religious instruction outside their homes. Religious officials were

> treated as declassed members of society, which involved sharp discrimination in securing housing, always extremely limited in food rations and jobs, as well as in the admission of their children to schools.[10]

In the battle to purge religion from the Russian psyche, the Orthodox Church, the state religion of Tsarist Russia, also came under attack. The aim here, however, was not so much its instant abolition but rather the hope that, when curtailed sufficiently, it would wither and die a natural death. On February 5, 1918, the government announced the "separation of the Church from the state and from the schools." The ancient marriage and divorce laws were repealed. Henceforth only civil marriage was to be officially recognized. Illegitimacy was to entail no disabilities. Divorce would be granted upon request of either partner.

Though rabbis and other synagogue functionaries were officially placed on a par with the religious leaders of other faiths, in reality they suffered much more severely since they lacked the backing of a well-organized national church body. Jewish religious leaders experienced far greater persecution that their Christian compatriots, and most of their synagogues were padlocked by governmental decree.

Generally it was the Jewish Communists who were the most outspoken opponents of religion. Foremost among them was Emelian Yaroslavskii, who became the President of the Russian Godless Society which embarked on an atheistic propaganda campaign throughout the Soviet Union with the full support of Lenin and his government. In 1932, the Society had a membership of

---

[10]Baron, *The Russian Jew*, p. 211.

5,500,000. Article 124 of its constitution stated: "Freedom for the conduct of religious worship and freedom for anti-religious propaganda is recognized for all citizens." It clearly meant that while one could not proselitize religiously, everyone was perfectly free to spread anti-religious propaganda with every means at his disposal. In its program, the Communist Party expressed the hope that the Godless Society would realize its endeavors

> in the complete withering away of religious prejudice. The party strives towards a complete destruction of the relation between the exploiting class and the organization of religious propaganda, thus effecting the actual liberation of the toiling mass from religious prejudice, and towards organizing a most extensive scientific, educational and anti-religious propaganda.[11]

At the same time the Party advised its followers not to insult the believers' feelings, "since that would only lead to the strengthening of religious fanaticism."

The anti-religious strictures of Lenin's government had a far more deleterious effect upon the Jews than upon their non-Jewish neighbors. For two millennia, religion had been the primary pillar of Jewish survival. Now the question arose as to whether the Jewish community could long endure without the firm anchor of its religious moorings. Most Russian Jews still adhered to the rituals and ceremonies of their Jewish faith. Their children studied, for the most part, in religiously oriented schools. Now these youngsters would be compelled to attend secular classes that would present the teachings of Communism as a religion and a way of life.

Against this background the ideological battle between the Yiddishists and the Hebraists about the primacy of their respective languages in Jewish cultural life was fought. First the Jewish communists and then Lenin's government denounced Hebrew as the "language of the Jewish bourgeoisie, religion and Zionism,

[11]Julius F. Hecker, *Religion and Communism: A Study of Religion and Atheism in Russia* (London, 1933), p. 275.

and hence, as an instrument of counterrevolution." Within a few
years Hebrew language and literature were limited to a few
classrooms at universities, where they were taught as part of the
dead cultures of the ancient Near East. Indeed, under such totalitarian pressures, it is little wonder that the Hebrew poet Elisha
Rudin wrote an epitaph for Hebrew culture in the Soviet Union:

> On the rivers of sorrow they stifled our song,
> The song of Zion, crystalline and bright,
> Made old and young alike forget our tongue,
> Snuffed out its sparkles of splendor and light.
> On rivers of sorrow our tongue was slain,
> How can I ever forget my shame?
> The cup of our sufferings, the honor's stain,
> All that I swallowed in the Sorrow's name."[12]

Both Lenin and the Jewish communists believed that sup-
pressing the practice of Judaism, prohibiting the use of the Hebrew language in any form, and destroying synagogues and Jewish establishments would compel the Jews to assimilate. Lenin
sought to accelerate this assimilative process still further by encouraging Jewish agricultural colonization. Assimilation was also
abetted by the mass departures of Jews from the Ukraine to such
urban centers as Moscow and Leningrad in the wake of the pogroms in the Ukraine and White Russia during the Civil War between the Bolsheviks and their opponents.

Jewish leaders became convinced that their people would become assimilated if they continued to depart from the Pale of
Jewish Settlement of Tsarist times. This point was emphasized
by Maria Y. Frumkin, a leading spokesman of the Party at the
Six (and last) All Union Conference of the Jewish Sections which
met in Moscow in December, 1926.

> Very likely the process of assimilation will engulf all the
> national minorities scattered in the cities. . . . Consider-
> ing the probability of such assumilation, we must, by

---

[12]Elisha Rudin, *Bi-Fe'at Nekhar* (Tel Aviv, 1938), pp. 23, 38. See also Baron,
The Russian Jew, p. 213.

our approach, indoctrinate the Jewish workers and
leaders not to judge each particular activity from the
standpoint of national self-preservation, but rather from
that of its usefulness to socialist reconstruction.[13]

Another major factor in the rate of assimilation was the spiral-
ing rate of intermarriage which, within a few years, reached
twenty-five percent of Jewish marriages in the interior of Russia.

Lenin's New Economic Policy (NEP) and the Jews

In 1921 the economy of Soviet Russia lay in ruins. Seven years
of war and civil war had produced catastrophe. Industrial production stood at thirteen percent of prewar volume. The grain
harvest had fallen from 74 million tons in 1916 to 30 million tons
in 1919 and continued to decline still further. Inflation was ramp-
ant, and the Communists, although they hated and feared it, continued to contribute to it by printing paper money. Lenin presented a new economic policy to alleviate these economic ills.

The NEP was a series of measures designed to eliminate the
excesses of war communism, "to foster the alliance between the
workers and the peasants and to create conditions which would
favor greater production." Its primary purpose was the restoration
of a degree of economic autonomy within the framework of a
socialist economy. The first NEP measure was a tax-in-kind on
farmers in place of requisitions. Farmers were permitted to dis-
pose of their produce as they wished, and were not compelled to
join collectives. Small businessmen were also granted similar
measures of economic freedom. Although the government re-
tained the ownership of banks, railways and the largest enterprises, private entrepreneurs were permitted to resume the management of smaller concerns, to hire labor, and to trade more or
less freely with the goods they produced.

This new era of "free enterprise" benefited the peasants, the
small businessmen and the industrial workers. Slowly the economy
began to revive under the NEP.

The NEP also served as a boon to the Jews since it abolished

---

[13]Baron, *The Russian Jew*, p. 213.

many discriminatory fiscal laws that had previously restricted them. Before its instigation, the economic position of the Jews had assumed catastrophic proportions. Fully one-third of the Jews had sunk into the mire of "declassed" persons since they were the petty businessmen, artisans and craftsmen who were labelled socially undesirable after the Bolshevik Revolution. Now, the NEP became a transitional period for the Jews in readjusting to the Communist line of economic thinking.

In summarizing Lenin's relationship to the Jews, one may say that, though he may have been influenced by Marx's anti-Semitic statements, Lenin explicitly opposed anti-Semitism on both theoretical and practical grounds. However, in matters of religion, Zionism and Hebrew culture, Lenin advocated a policy of total destruction and assimilation. Systematic destruction of synagogues and mass deportations of religious leaders to Siberia were undertaken. Lenin was aided by the Jewish Communists who had forsaken their Jewish heritage for the sake of Communism and atheism.

It would seem that, despite his avowed tolerance, Lenin carried out in practice much of Marx's theoretical solutions to "the Jewish problem." History, as it pertains to the spiritual, cultural and communal plight of Soviet Jewry, must hold Lenin responsible for the actions that provided the example for future Soviet leaders like Stalin, Khrushchev and Brezhnev to emulate. To be sure, Lenin also advocated the slow dying process of all organized religion and the religious institutions of other faiths as well. Nevertheless, the destructive process against Judaism and its institutions took place with thoroughness and a lightening-like rapidity. Lenin's bequest to Stalin was a heritage of continuing the process of assimilating the Jews and destroying the religious institutions which had served as their rock and refuge through centuries of persecution under the Tsars.

CHAPTER FIVE

STALIN AND THE JEWS

One of Stalin's major contributions to socialism was his concept of socialism in one country. Prior to his taking power, it had been generally accepted by socialists that to be successful a revolution should take place simultaneously in several advanced countries. The fact that the socialist revolution took place in an agricultural, backward country like Russia was disturbing, but the Communists believed that revolution in western countries was imminent. Stalin, who possessed only a mediocre capacity for theoretical thinking, had originally shared this view, but changed his mind at the end of 1924. He developed the thesis that a socialist system could be built in one country, provided that that country had a large territory, large population and abundant natural resources.

Stalin's socialism in one country was used as the chief weapon against Leon Trotsky and, more important, it became the theoretical basis of Soviet planned economy. Stalin held that the assurance that a socialist society could be built in the Soviet Union was the essential prerequisite for the vast program of industrialization and collectivization embarked upon under the successive Five Year Plans. In a sense, the acceptance of socialism in one country was the triumph of nationalism over internationalism in the evolution of Communist doctrine, Trotsky was a Westerner among Russian revolutionaries and thought in terms of European revolutions. To Stalin, however, who had little foreign experience, the Russian revolution came first, and its progress should not depend upon what happened in the international arena.

Willingly or otherwise, the Jews in Stalin's Russia had to adjust to socialism in one country. The Five Year Plan was responsible for a significant transformation in Russian Jewish life. The immense process of industrializing backward Russia within a few decades absorbed the energies of countless thousands of Jews. For the first time many Jewish workers had become proletarians working with machines in the factories and mines and working, too, for State wages.

Since socialism in one country was nationalistic in its scope, anti-Semitism found its way to the surface during periods of turmoil and fed upon nationalist emotions and hatred.[1] Stalin never hesitated to exploit anti-Jewish tendencies in his struggle with his opposition. At first, by dark hints and allusions, Stalin's agents stirred up anti-Semitic prejudice and brought it nearer the surface until it reached its climax during the period of the great purges in 1937-1939. The anti-Semitism was so virulent and all-encompassing during this time that Trotsky, usually reticent on the subject, could hardly contain himself and wrote in a letter to Bukharin in March, 1926:

> . . . is it true, it is possible that in our party, in Moscow, in workers' cells, anti-Semitic agitation should be carried on with impunity?

To the same indignant question asked at a Politburo meeting a fortnight later, he received no answer. It was a fact that, among the leaders of Stalin's opposition, Jews played an important role. Among the most prominent of them were Trotsky himself, Kamenev and Zinoviev. Stalin's agitators labeled them "rootless cosmopolitans"—people who did not care for socialism in one country, in their own fatherland. So pervasive was their hypocrisy that the word "Jew" was not used, but the point in those denunciations of "rootless cosmopolitans" was well taken.[2]

On the other hand, one could find many Jews among Stalin's followers. For example, at the head of the forcible collectivization in the Ukraine was the Jew Lazar M. Kaganovich. It is in this juxtaposition that one can see the tragic imbroglio in which the

---

[1] Isaac Deutscher, "The Russian Revolution and the Jewish Problem," in *The Non-Jewish Jew* (London, 1968), p. 75.
[2] *Ibid.*

Jews were trapped. In town they were persecuted as "rootless cosmopolitans" opposed to socialism in Russia; in the countryside they were despised by the peasants, who saw in the communist Kaganovich their chief oppressor. To these contradictions were soon added others. The petty trader, the speculator, the *luft-mensch,* became a common stereotype of the Jews, at the same time that Jewish professors, doctors, teachers and other were contributing much to the development and modernization of Russia. The contradictions inherent in the changing Soviet society tended to affect the Jewish population more sharply and cruelly than they affected any other ethnic or national group in the USSR.

Stalin's rule can be divided into three periods: the Pre-War Era (1924-1939); the Second World War Era (1939-1945); and the Post-War Era (1945-1953). We will look at Stalin's policies toward Jews during those three periods.

The Pre-War Era (1924-1939)

The mass settlement of Jews in agricultural communes assumed primary significance during the Pre-War Era. As the Tsar had done a century earlier, Stalin's government put land in the Ukraine and the Crimea at the disposal of settlers, requiring only that these agricultural colonists bear the cost of equipping and establishing themselves. A Jewish commission known as the Komzet was formed and under the direction of a non-Jewish People's Commissar, Smidovich, it speedily bent to the task of settling the Jews upon the land. Working with the Komzet was a private Jewish organization called the Ozet. Many Jews responded enthusiastically to the call to return to the soil. Generous assistance was provided to those who were willing to forsake the comforts of an urban civilization for the uncertain vicissitudes of farming in the provinces. Further aid was forthcoming to these twentieth century Russian pioneers in the form of supplementary assistance from a Joint Distribution Committee. The cry "back to the land" was eagerly taken up and, in a short while, 50,000 persons were resettled and earning their living as farmers, agricultural workers or rural handicraftsmen. Among their numbers were formerly disenchanted youth, men and women of all ages, and old city dwellers. All shared the satisfactions of living and working in a rural environment.

The work was strange and tiring, especially for the women, and life on the frontier was hard. But each person had the profound satisfaction of living and working on his own plot of land and each could look to the future with hope. In the tranquility of the country, the Russian Jew could achieve a spiritual contentment and fulfill his religious longings more meaningfully than he had been able to do in the noisy city.

In 1927 the Komzet sought to turn Jewish nationalist longings to the advantage of Russia by advocating a Jewish agricultural settlement in the area of Biro-Bidzhan.[3] The Komzet leaders effectively used nationalist arguments in their appeals to Jews and sought to undermine the powerful Zionist sentiment among the Jewish masses by proposing an alternate homeland in Russia itself. Zionism, the Jewish masses were told, was a tool of British imperialism, while the Biro-Bidzhan scheme was a means of meeting the great economic need of Jewish restratification and stabilization of Jewish life as a territorially-rooted nationality, similar to the other nationalities in the Soviet Union.

Biro-Bidzhan, which covered an area the size of Connecticut and Massachusetts combined, was eminently suitable for this purpose. Jewish settlers would not have to displace any native population since there were only some thirty thousand inhabitants in that district. Soviet propagandists effectively contrasted Zionism, which attempted to impose Jewish rule upon a large Arab population in Palestine, with Biro-Bidzhan, which did not present the Jews with such a problem.

> That is why (wrote M. Seme in December, 1934) we have in Palestine mutual pogroms between Jews and Arabs, Arab delegations appearing before the English High Commissioner against Jews, and Jewish delegations arguing against the Arabs. At the first assembly in the Jewish autonomous region, (on the contrary) we had delegates of workers in collective farms from among

---

[3]Baron, *The Russian Jew,* p. 231.

all the people of the Soviet Union and we thus (generated) a new wave of international brotherhood. For this reason Zionism is a basis for counterrevolution and reaction among Jews, a meeting place for all their black faschist and clerical elements, whereas around the Jewish autonomous region are centered all the sympathies of the progressive and revolutionary elements in the Jewish masses of capitalist lands.[4]

Simeon Dimanshtain, the Jewish Commissar, was careful to deny the nationalist origins of the proposed settlement upon its being approved on March 30, 1928. He stated that:

> We need a compact Jewish settlement not for any kind of nationalist purposes, from which we are far removed, but for the sake of concrete goals which are connected with the general upbuilding of socialism in our country. Under healthier cultural and economic conditions, the Jewish masses will be transformed into competent and exemplary builders of the new socialist life. Toward this goal we ought to work energetically while combating all nationalistic tendencies.[5]

Colonization was begun in Biro-Bidzhan in 1928 and during the first three very difficult years only a few thousand Jews, mostly artisans and workingmen from small Ukrainian and Byelorussian towns settled there. They endured great hardships in acclimating themselves to the desolate region. A small group of pioneering Jewish Communist leaders volunteered to help the workers build their new towns and villages. These leaders, headed by Professor Lieberg of Kiev, were extremely successful in stimulating the progress of the Biro-Bidzhan scheme. They motivated the Jews to share in the noble effort which, they noted, was as significant to the Soviet Union as it was to the colonists themselves. Despite their support and encouragement many of the

---

[4]Baron, *The Russian Jew*, p. 232.
[5]*Ibid.*, p. 231.

pioneers were unable to endure the strain and abandoned the project.

When the Japanese invaded Manchuria in 1931, Stalin assigned top priority to settlements along the borders of China. After three years of indecision the concept of a Jewish settlement in Biro-Bidzhan was given new impetus by the government and in 1934 the Supreme Soviet formally declared Biro-Bidzhan an autonomous Jewish region. This declaration won the friendship of many Jews, especially since Hitler and his Nazi regime had already begun its nefarious persecution of Jews. By the end of 1935 some fourteen thousand Jews were living in the autonomous region and comprised about a quarter of the population. They had their own collective farms and were active in industry, manufacturing, public service and administration. Jews established kindergartens, primary, secondary and vocational schools, and research institutes. Most of the instruction was in Yiddish, some was bilingual—Yiddish and Russian. Initial steps were taken to start a Yiddish publishing house, a Jewish press, a Yiddish theater, and various cultural and artistic groups. Then, in 1936, Stalin initiated his great and terrifying purges. Under his rule, the pervasive fear of the informer and the secret police had made the air heavy with suspicion and distrust. His defense of terror was voiced in an interview with a visiting foreign workers' delegation on November 5, 1927.

> We are a country surrounded by capitalist states. The internal enemies of our revolution are the agents of the capitalists of all countries. . . . In fighting against the enemies at home, we fight the counterrevolutionary elements of all countries. . . . No, comrades, we do not wish to repeat the mistakes of the Parisian Communards. The GPU (a military-political tribunal) is necessary for the Revolution and will continue to exist to the terror of the enemies of the proletariat.[6]

---

[6]Merle Fainsod, "Terror as a System of Power," *How Russia is Ruled* (Cambridge, Mass., 1962), p. 423.

The full significance of Stalin's theory did not materialize until the period of the great purges when the execution of the Old Bolsheviks clearly demonstrated that the paramount role of terror in Stalinist ideology was to serve as a bulwark for his own monopoly of party leadership.[7]

At the height of the purge of 1937, Stalin tried to justify mass terror on the grounds that the internal class struggle was becoming more and more acute as the Soviet Union moved toward socialism. Khrushchev was later to condemn this claim in his secret speech to the Twentieth Party Congress, but he did not reject that part of Stalin's theory which stressed the danger from without.

During 1935 the purge gathered momentum, but its scope was still relatively restricted. Beginning February 1, 1936, all old party cards were to be exchanged for new cards; the issuance of new cards was to unmask the enemies who had survived the earlier screenings.[8] Party membership declined from 2,807,786 in January, 1934 to 2,044,412 in April, 1936.[9] The purges culminated during 1936-1938. The most dramatic manifestation was the series of show trials in which every vestige of Old Bolshevik opposition leadership was officially discredited and exterminated. The first of the great public trials took place in August, 1936. Two of the leading Jewish Bolsheviks, Kamenev and Zimoviev, together with fourteen others, were charged with organizing a secret terrorist center under instructions from Trotsky, accomplishing the murder of Kirov, and plotting similar attempts against the lives of other party leaders. These two leaders, who were among the first close comrades of Lenin and who contributed much to the Bolshevik Revolution, were executed. When Marshal M. N. Tuckhachevskii stood trial for conspiring with the Germans, the Jewish general Jan Gamarnik, chief of the army's Political Administration, committed suicide. At the Eighteenth Party Congress of 1939, Gamarnik's successor, L. Mekhlis, spoke of the "Gamarnik-Bulin gang of spies" who had done their greatest damage by appointing traitors to the high levels of the officers' corps.

---

[7]Ibid.
[8]Fainsod, *How Russia is Ruled*, p. 435.
[9]Ibid.

The great purges wreaked terrible havoc upon all who felt their wrath. Mass executions were followed by the total suppression of Jewish cultural life. Fear and terror filed the hearts of every Jew in Russia, from the humblest citizen to the ranking Communist Party leader. No longer was anti-Semitism regarded as a criminal offense. Instead, it became almost the official policy of Stalin and his regime. Even before the Second World War the institutions of Yiddish culture were on the verge of ruin. In 1933, for example, Jewish book titles reached a record peak of 668, but in 1934 this number dropped to 348. Bibliographical statistics concerning the cultural attrition between the years 1935-1939 are considered unreliable at best.

Even during the purges, Stalin continued his anti-religious crusade unabated. At the Conference of 1936 the All Union Party adopted the following resolutions:

> Among the tasks of the cultural revolution, embracing the widest masses, special place is occupied by the struggle against the opiate of the people—religion—a struggle which must be carried on systematically and relentlessly. . . . At the same time the proletarian power, allowing freedom of confession and destroying the privileged position of the former state religion, conducts by all possible means anti-religious propaganda, and reconstructs all upbringing and educational work on the basis of a scientific, materialistic world-view.[10]

In a letter of 1930 Rabbis Israel Meir Kagan and Hayyim Ozer Grodzenski, two prominent religious leaders, wrote that the Holy Scrolls, books of the Talmud, phylacteries, and the scrolls at the door posts had been burned in the streets. Ritual baths were shut down and the observance of the family-purity laws was rapidly being abandoned. The Communists forced Jews to desecrate the Sabbath. Many of the rabbis and Torah scholars were being sentenced to prison, and many others were banished to

---

[10]Paul Anderson, *People, Church, and State in Modern Russia* (New York, 1944), p. 62.

Siberia.[11] In 1932 a central anti-religious museum in Moscow opened a special Jewish department, satirizing the "stupidities" of Judaism. As a rule, it was the vindictive Jewish Communists who went to the most perfidious extremes; preparing public banquets on Yom Kippur, and conducting mock trials of Jewish "bourgeois" patriarchs during the Passover seder in order to show their contempt for the "superstition" of Jewish practices.

As an entire generation of young people matured in this atheistic society, Jewish religious loyalties faded rapidly. By 1934 and 1936 Stalin could afford to be content believing, correctly in part, that the new generation had been completely "emancipated" from religion and could repeal some of the harshest anti-religious legislation.

With their ethnic individuality under assault, and their cultural and religious loyalties ridiculed and largely destroyed, the Jews were perhaps more to be pitied than in the days of the Tsar. No longer were they persecuted as Jews, but as generations passed, the historic beliefs and traditions that made life meaningful to them throughout the centuries were being inexorably eroded.

With the onset of these purges Biro-Bidzhan fell victim to a savage blow from which it never recovered. The leaders of Biro-Bidzhan were charged with being Trotskyites, nepotists, nationalists and Zionists and were obliterated. Dismissed from their jobs, many were imprisoned, exiled or executed, including Professor Lieberg, the most beloved of all, who disappeared and was secretly slain. Most Jewish teachers, journalists and writers were also discharged, arrested and imprisoned. Foreign volunteers were accused of espionage; of conspiring with the Zionists and the international Jewish bourgeoisie to spy for the imperialist powers and to commit sabotage. Many were imprisoned and put to death.

There is no doubt that Stalin's government had decided that the project of settling Jews on the Chinese border was impractical and should not be allowed to develop. Nevertheless, after the purges the plan was maintained through sheer inertia and there

---

[11]Letter from Rabbis Kagan and Grodzenski, Adar, 1930, in *Michtevei Hafets Hayyim* (New York, 1953), p. 57.

was even an increase in population. But Biro-Bidzhan functioned as a leaderless body without specific aims and goals.

The Second World War Era (1939-1945)

Oddly enough World War Two brought a new spark of life to Biro-Bidzhan. Exploiting the publicity value of the Jewish Autonomous Region in the Western countries, the Soviet government allowed the Jewish settlers to appeal to world Jewry to safeguard the future of Russian Jews by aiding the Red army. Once again, Jews began to settle in Biro-Bidzhan. Some were refugees from countries annexed by the Soviet Union, others were fleeing from the German invaders. There were among the new settlers some dedicated Communists who tried to restore a modicum of leadership to the region.

Second World War (1939-1945)

During the short period of detente between Hitler and Stalin at the start of the Second World War, Jews in Russia were subjected to intensified persecution as Hitler's racism added to Stalin's anti-Semitism. The gifted foreign minister, Maxim Litvinov, resigned and was replaced by the pure Aryan Vyacheslav Molotov since only an Aryan could sign a treaty with the Germans. Stalin and Molotov sent messages to Hitler promising a friendship cemented by blood and Stalin announced his willingness to help Hitler liberate the Ukrainians from Polish oppression.

Hitler's subsequent invasion of the Ukraine was met at first with relief and even joy among Ukrainians. After the violent upheavals that had engulfed Russia prior to the war—the bestial brutalities of forced collectivization, the terrible purges, the mass deportations to concentration camps, tensions in Russia "were so acute and dangerous that at the beginning of the war the whole structure—moral, economic, political—seemed on the brink of collapse."[12] But it was soon apparent that Stalin at his worse was better than Hitler.

---

[12]Isaac Deutscher, "The Russian Revolution and the Jewish Question," in *The Non-Jewish Jew,* p. 76.

As the German-Russian detente collapsed,

> The age-old prejudice, always smoldering, sometimes
> damped down, but never extinguished, burst out; and
> the Nazis fanned it into a terrible flame. Stalin and his
> government on their part were afraid that the war
> against the Nazis might be seen by the Ukrainians and
> the Russians as a war fought just in defense of the Jews.[13]

The Nazis convinced many Ukrainians and Russians that
"This war is a Jewish intrigue. You are fighting the war in the
interest of the Jews." Russian soldiers were treated with Nazi
propaganda that included specific data:

> . . . facing a regiment recruited from a certain area, the
> Nazis blared over their loudspeakers and radios names
> of prominent Jews from that area and then asked the
> Soviet soldiers whether the Jews were among them, or
> else had shirked their military duty and stayed behind
> to enrich themselves through war speculation.[14]

For the most part, the Jewish names were those of prominent
citizens who, for that very reason, were known to the recruits.
The fact that these prominent Jewish citizens were over-age or
badly needed behind the front "because of their expertness in
the production of war materials or for other vital government serv-
ices, was hardly considered by the unsophisticated *muzhiks* now
in uniforms." In other effective broadcasts, the Nazi propagandists
warned the Soviet soldiers not to entrust their lives to "Yankel
Kreiser," that is, to Lt. General Jacob Kreiser, one of the prominent Jewish war heroes. However, the facts bear witness that
during the Second World War the regular Russian Army decorated 34,000 Jewish soldiers for bravery in combat. The Jews
were the fourth largest national group in the Red Army to merit
such recognition although they ranked only seventh in size of
population. More than 100 Jewish soldiers were awarded the
title, "Hero of the Soviet Union." Among the outstanding indi-

---

13*Ibid.*, p. 77.
14Baron, *The Russian Jew*, p. 302.

viduals thus cited was Captain Israel Fisanovich who, as a submarine commander, sank 13 enemy ships, and also earned an American Navy Cross. A woman flier, Lt. Lily Litvak, distinguished herself at Stalingrad and shot down 6 German planes at Orel before losing her own life.

Despite these heroic exploits, Jewish combatants occasionally suffered from anti-Semitism among both Soviet officers and enlisted men. Thus, the number of decorated Jewish soldiers is perhaps lower than it might have been had not some Jewish soldiers been "passed over because of the pernicious influence of the late Supreme Army Commissar Scherbakov, member of the Politbureau . . . and dyed-in-the-wool anti-Semite," according to a later report by a Jewish captain.[15]

Stalin's response to this propaganda was twofold. On the one hand he continued his own government's harsh policies toward the Jews, arresting, for example, thousands of businessmen from Soviet-occupied Poland. Many were exiled to Siberia and other remote places, some were killed, some tortured, and others offered Stalin's method of "rehabilitation." In 1939 the author's father, an entrepreneur who bought cattle, slaughtered it in accordance with ritual law, and sold the kosher meat to Jews, was arrested for exploiting the masses and continuing a religious ritual which had to be uprooted. The author and his mother and 3 sisters were also sent to Siberia to experience hunger, homelessness and the Siberian cold for five fatherless years. The author's father was treated with Stalin's rehabilitation—which in his case meant not seeing his family, subsisting on water and a piece of bread daily and cutting trees from early morning until late at night.[16]

On the other hand, Stalin did all he could to play down the realities of Nazi anti-Semitism in his own war propaganda, lest his government be justly accused of fighting in defense of the Jews.

You had, therefore, the very curious phenomenon that throughout the Second World War the Soviet press

---

[15]*Ibid.*, p. 303.

[16]The author's personal experiences during this time will be found in a volume now in preparation.

hardly ever reported on the fate of the Jews, hardly ever
mentioned Auschwitz and Majdanek.[17]

Nazi atrocities were reported to the Russian people, but the mass
murders of civilians was played down—perhaps because it might
have proved difficult to explain the Red army's retreat into the
interior, leaving masses of Russians unprotected. The specific
Nazi annihilation of millions of Jews was completely ignored in
Russian reporting.

There was, indeed, a third aspect to Stalin's response to
Hitler's anti-Semitism, and that is his attempts to put it to his
own use in enlisting aid from other nations. Two Polish socialist
refugees, Hanryk Erlich and Viktor Alter, conceived of a Jewish
Anti-Fascist Committee that might carry out pro-Soviet propaganda in the Western Jewish communities. When news of the
suggestion reached Stalin his first response was to have the two
men shot—apparently simply because he was reminded that these
two former leaders of the hated Second International were still
alive. He then proceeded to implement their plan. The prominent
Jewish actor, Solomon Mikhoels, a leader in the Jewish theater,
and the Yiddish poet Itzik Fefer, traveled from coast to coast in
America enlisting the support and sympathy of the American
Jewish community. Paralleling this, Stalin permitted a relaxation
of anti-Jewish activity in Russia. Yiddish newspapers reappeared,
cultural institutions re-opened and publishing activities resumed.
The Jewish Anti-Fascist Committee numbered among its members leading writers, including Ilya Ehrenburg, Red Army gen-
erals, and scientists. The committee continued its activity after
the Second World War by issuing reports depicting the anti-
Jewish atrocities of the Nazis in the Soviet Union.

As we have seen, it was at this time also that Biro-Bidzhan
was given new life—primarily for the publicity value it might
offer.

Ironically, Stalin's policy of arrest and deportation as well as
his subtle use of the Biro-Bidzhan scheme, saved the lives of two
and a half million Jews. Forcibly and hastily removed from the

---

[17]Deutscher, "The Russian Revolution and the Jewish Question," p. 77.

invaded areas, the Jews were uprooted from their homes, forced to eke out a meager living, and again became prominent in the black market, producing new waves of anti-Semitism on the grounds of exploitation. But whatever the agony of their existence and the extremes of poverty that brought them once more into a position that could easily fan the flames of prejudice, they were saved from Hitler's concentration camps and his crematoria at Auschwitz and Treblinka.

The Post-War Era (1945-1953)

During the post-war period the nerves of the country were again stretched taut. To the chaos, weariness and exhaustion of a devastating war was added, in 1946, a catastrophic failure of the harvest such as Russia had not seen in more than half a century. Famine was widespread and so was despair when the Russian people realized what it meant to have lost twenty million men in the fighting. Not a man could be seen on the Russian fields and farms: only women, old men and children, tilling the soil and nurturing the meager crops which could hardly provide sustenance for the nation. All restrictions on the employment of juvenile labor were lifted and work and overwork by everyone available was the rule.

During this time of troubles, sharp and painful clashes between the old and new antagonisms once more occurred. The epic struggle between the two conflicting currents in the Russian mentality and ideology of Soviet society, the struggle between nationalism and internationalism was once more debated.

> . . . if one does not bear constantly in mind the fact that this struggle constitutes the basic phenomenon of Soviet society, one misses the key to the understanding of the history of the Stalin period, of the events which followed it, and of the place which the Jewish problem occupies in Soviet life. You have nationalists and anti-Semites among the peasants, the workers, the bureaucracy, the intelligentsia. You have internationalists and therefore enemies of anti-Semitism in all these layers of society as well.[18]

The year 1948, on the other hand, was yet another tragic year for Soviet Jewry. Once again Stalin used his savage guillotine to purge those without recourse to justice. Almost all the members of the Jewish Anti-Fascist Committee were executed, as was Deputy Commissar for Foreign Affairs Solomon Lozovsky. They were accused of conspiring to detach the Crimea and establish a separate Jewish state. The paranoid origin of this Stalinist suppression apparently lay in a suggestion by Lozovsky that survivors from the Western Ukraine and Byelorussia might be provided with resettlement areas in the Crimea, from which Stalin had forcibly removed the Tatar inhabitants on charges of disloyalty during the Nazi occupation.

It was in 1948 also that Biro-Bidzhan was once more a victim of Stalin's whims. This time the Soviet authorities were not satisfied merely to exile and execute the Jewish elite. This time they did not cease until they had uprooted every vestige of Jewish culture. Every Jewish school, every publishing house, and every theater was closed. The number of Jews in administration and local government was curtailed. There has not been a single Jewish school in Biro-Bidzhan since 1948; nor has there been a single Jewish class for the teaching of Yiddish. There remain no Jewish theaters and no institutions for the dissemination of Jewish culture.

Upon leaving Biro-Bidzhan, even after speaking to living healthy Jews, one begins to feel as though he has left a cemetery where every legend reads: "Here lies a Jewish dream, born in 1928, died in 1948, after a long illness and prolonged agony. May its soul rest in peace amidst the great pioneering schemes."

For five years the blood bath continued unabated. From 1948 to 1953 anti-Semitism became an official though unacknowledged policy. More than 400 Jewish writers, poets, journalists, scholars, and artisans were arrested, exiled or executed. The sudden death of the prominent Jewish actor Solomon Mikhoels was explained as a result of an automobile accident. Such nonsense cannot be accepted by anyone who witnessed hundreds of important Jewish leaders arrested, tortured and killed. The imaginations of

---

[18]Deutscher, "The Russian Revolution and the Jewish Problem," pp. 79ff.

Stalin and his followers were constantly at work to conjure up false excuses for their shedding of innocent blood. In April, 1949, the free world was shattered by the sudden announcement of the jailing of the five most eminent Yiddish writers, David Bergelson, Samuel Halkin, Peretz Markish, Der Nister and Itzik Fefer. While Bergelson was found guilty of Pro-Israel tendencies, no charges were presented in the other cases. Certainly no one could incriminate Fefer for lack of Soviet patriotism. Fefer had not only served as a colonel in the Red Army during the Second World War, but had proclaimed himself through his poetry to be a loyal and proud Russian. More than any other Russian poet he distinguished himself in his patriotic diatribes, and was now languishing in prison as a traitor to the Fatherland. These arrests were followed by a number of others and, before long, practically all Yiddish literary leaders were incarcerated. Quota systems were introduced for the admissions of Jews to educational and other institutions. Jews were banned from the supper echelons of the Soviet army, the Foreign Ministry and the Communist Party.

Stalin's anti-Semitic inclinations were made manifest as his life neared its end. In January, 1953, it was announced that a group of Kremlin physicians, most of them Jews, had conspired through the instigation of Zionist organizations and British and American intelligence agencies in a plot against Kremlin led leadership. Stalin, it was later learned from his heirs, talked wildly of exiling the entire Russian Jewish community to Siberia.

When Stalin died in 1953, his successors announced that the doctors' plot was a frame-up and called an abrupt halt to the spread of officially-encouraged anti-Semitism. The question then arose as to whether Stalin's successors would be successful in eradicating the tide of anti-Semitism, encouraged and nurtured for so many years by Stalin. Even if they could be successful in curbing government sponsored anti-Semitism, there could be no guarantee that the masses of Russian people could expunge from their hearts and minds the vitriolic lessons that Stalin had taught so effectively for so many years.

CHAPTER SIX

KHRUSHCHEV AND THE JEWS

Nikita Sergeevich Khrushchev, a ruthless and ambitious Communist, was not originally considered a serious contender for the position he ultimately came to fill—successor to Stalin.

Born in 1894 in Kalinovka, just northeast of the Ukrainian border, Khrushchev was the son of a miner and held several jobs as a shepherd, locksmith and mechanic. He joined the party in 1918, fought in the Civil War, and studied briefly at the University of Kharkov and later at the Industrial Academy of Moscow. Possessing a flamboyant, outgoing personality, Khrushchev quickly manifested a highly skilled capacity for party management and embarked upon a career as a political organizer. In 1934, he became Kaganovich's assistant in running the Moscow Party organization and the following year succeeded him as its secretary. In 1938, he headed the Ukrainian Party, and, except for 1946-47 when Kaganovich replaced him briefly, he remained in that position until 1949. In 1949 he returned to Moscow where he once again assumed command of the Party and became a secretary of the Central Committee. Continuing his political climb, Khrushchev became a member of the presidium of the Communist Party when it was reorganized in 1952, first secretary in 1953, and chairman of the Council of Ministers in 1958.

Khrushchev, unlike Stalin, was an advocate of change. He initiated numerous reforms, altered the structure of industry and farming, reformed the schools and the social security system, and frequently visited foreign countries. Though primarily a man of action rather than a theoretician, he did revise some Communist doctrines. Like Lenin, Khrushchev never doubted "the righteousness and wisdom of his opinions and had clear-cut and unwaver-

53

ing views on subjects as far apart as plowing and corn growing, on the one hand, and painting, literature, and music, on the other."[1]

Khrushchev's attitude towards the Jews was shaped by his involvement in anti-Semitism in the Ukraine. Although most Ukrainians were satisfied merely with witnessing the Jews of Ukrainian towns decimated "as a result of the Nazis' rounding up all the Jewish inhabitants and mowing them down in ravines which thus became mass graves,"[2] a small minority collaborated with the Nazis and were even entrusted with guarding the infamous camps in which Jews were gassed. Although these latter Ukrainians constituted perhaps only a small minority of their people, the anti-Semitic propaganda in the Soviet Union nevertheless served as a constant stimulus for the Ukrainian dissidents.

The anti-Jewish propaganda of the Ukrainian secessionist elements was so vociferous that Khrushchev, while chairman of the Ukrainian Council of Peoples' Commissars and secretary of the Central Committee of the Commuist Party in the Ukraine, was compelled to appease the extreme nationalists. He secretly disposed of Jews in official positions in the Ukraine so as to assure the Ukranians that Soviet Ukraine was not "run by Jews." He decided that Jews were to be restricted to the barest minimum of municipal jobs. He systematically suppressed any specific mention of Jews as victims of Nazi barbarity in the Ukraine, "his purpose being to prevent their figuring in the war history of the Ukraine as the element which suffered most from the Germans during their occupation of the country."[3] He did not even permit the description of the largest massacre of Jews in the Ukraine, the mass executions at Babi Yar:

> . . . one of the largest of these massacres took place immediately outside Khrushchev's own city, Kiev, in a ravine known as Babi Yar, on September 29 and 30, 1941 where 33,771 Jews, men, women, and children were killed in two days, the shooting clearly audible in the

[1]Michael Florismky, *Russia a Short History* (N.Y. 1969), p. 589.
[2]Boris Smolar, *Soviet Jewry Today and Tomorrow* (N.Y., 1971), p. 28.
[3]*Ibid.*, p. 28.

center of the city . . . more than a million human beings, mostly Jews, were killed in the course of two years, very largely in Khrushchev's Ukraine.[4]

Naturally enough, the Russians had a great deal to say about German atrocities in general, "but they never made the Jews an issue. For years after the war, both during and after Khrushchev's rule, Kiev was a forbidden city: the only foreigners permitted entrance were a handful of UNRAA officials."[5] Edward Crankshaw, who served with the British Military Mission in Russia from 1941 to 1943 and is a correspondent for the *London Observer*, writes:

> But I remember very well, when I was first allowed to go there in 1955, asking the local director of Intourist to direct me to Babi Yar. At first he pretended he had never heard of Babi Yar. But when I insisted he said, 'Why do you want to go and look at a lot of dead Jews? If you're interested in Jews you'll see more than enough live ones on the streets.'[6]

No monument stands at Babi Yar, or, for that matter, at any place where the Jews were ruthlessly slaughtered. There was nothing to show that anything extraordinary had ever occurred there. To implement his policy of appeasing the extreme Ukrainian nationalists, Khrushchev ordered the construction of apartment buildings at the site of the covered ravine and the planting of woods there to obliterate this "episode" of mass murder from the memory of the Ukrainian people. Today, only a small, primitive stone marks the mass grave, and even this stone does not tell that the victims were Jews. Thus, Babi Yar remained a forbidden word until 1963, when the young poet Yevgeny Yevtushenko, incurred Khrushchev's intense wrath by writing his celebrated poem *Babi Yar,* in which he shamelessly confessed his share of guilt as a Russian.

---

[4]Edward Crankshaw, *Khrushchev: A Career* (New York, 1966), p. 154.
[5]*Ibid.,* pp. 154ff.
[6]*Ibid.,* p. 155.

With Stalin's death and Khrushchev's ascendancy to power, the Soviet Union entered into a new phase of political development. Once more the constant struggle between nationalism and internationalism became strikingly apparent. Stalin's death evoked a violent reaction against his chauvinism, anti-Semitism and nationalism and gave rise to internationalism's temporarily gaining the upper hand. But this was not the final triumph of internationalism once and for all. Far from it. There had been for years a shaky balance between the two trends and the balance had produced all the inconsistencies and changes in policies that we have seen. Tension appeared to ease briefly under Khrushchev, and the old rabbinical dream of a Yeshiva, a seminary for future rabbies, was realized in 1956 when the Moscow Synagogue was authorized to open its doors for a small school for higher religious education. A Hebrew prayer book was cleared for publication in an edition of 4,000 copies. There were reports that new synagogues were under construction and new assertion of Jewish community interests. But in 1957 the situation began to revert to "normal." Local officials were ordered to assume a stern posture toward their Jewish communities, the administrative strictures againt the Orthodox Church were applied with even greater severity against the synagogues. Some were closed down by atheist agitators; private prayer meetings were prohibited; and propagandists stepped up their virulent diatribes against the Jewish religion as a force for exploiting the working people.

A cogent political theory may be advanced for Khrushchev's suppression of Jewish community life during his rule. De-Stalinization, of course, was a primary philosophical goal of Khrushchev's regime. But in undertaking this campaign, he ran serious political risks by antagonizing the followers of Stalinist mentality in the Communist Party. He therefore refrained from lifting Stalin's sanctions against the Jewish community. Foreign analysts have speculated that this may have been an attempt by Khrushchev to go at least part way toward pacifying the neo-Stalinists in the party so he could carry on with de-Stalinization in other fields. Another reason for Khrushchev's suppression of the churches and synagogues was to combat the revival of interest in religion that flowered in 1959 among Soviet youth and such prominent dissident writers as Pasternak and Solzhenitsyn.[7] During the next five years, approximately half of the remaining 20,000 Orthodox Churches and all the monasteries, except for perhaps 15, were

---

[7]Since Solzhenitsyn has, during this writing, again been singled out by the Soviet Union for persecution in being deported from Russia in February, 1974, it would seem in place to offer a footnote here addressing itself to him. Solzhenitzyn's book, *The Gulag Archipelago, 1918-1956* is an historical account of the Soviet penal system. Incorporated in his prison camp study are personal experiences which portray for the first time the nature of forces that merged to form him as a critic of Stalinism and of the Kremlin system of rule by terror.

He was born in Kislovodsk in the North Caucasus on December 11, 1918 to liberal or radical parents. His father was a decorated officer in the Tsarist army who died before his son was born. His mother had great difficulty finding employment because of her bourgeois origins, so Alexander did not have an easy youth. But he proved himself a brilliant student and won rewards for his high mathematical skills. As he portrayed himself, "he was a patriotic youngster, filled with Young Communist zeal." (*New York Times,* December 31, 1973)

He believed in the teachings of Lenin but from the time he was 11 or 12 years old he began to develop a skepticism of Stalin after reading the first publicized trials in 1929 and 1930 of "wrecking" engineers, of the so-called "Promparty" and of the Mensheviks. His skepticism continued to grow during the 1930s but he continued to win high awards as a student and remained a faithful member of the Komsomol or Young Communist organization. He earned a degree in mathematics and physics from Rostov University and a second degree in writing in a correspondence course offered by a Moscow literature institute. He was married in 1940 and drafted into the army, serving as a soldier in a horsedrawn transport unit in 1941. After 6 months he was sent to an officers' training school and then to the front as the commander of an artillery battery. He experienced at first hand the unpreparedness, disorder and leadership errors that brought Russia to the brink of disaster and his suspicion of Stalin's leadership "intensified as a result of the terrible defeats inflicted on the Soviet Union in the first months of the war." (*The New York Times,* December 31, 1973)

In correspondence with a close friend serving on another front the two agreed that the trouble was Stalin. Their correspondence, containing thinly veiled criticism of Stalin, was intercepted and the author and his friend were arrested.

Thus began a long reassessment of Russian history and the part he himself would play in it. Remaining faithful to Communism and the Soviet system, he allowed himself to question what he had been taught since his youth.

> "This agonizing process went forward as he himself experienced the most painful kinds of torments, particularly before and after his assignment for several years to a 'sharashka,' a secret prison scientific laboratory in which he worked for a time because of his talent in mathematics and physics. (*The New York Times,* December 31, 1973)

Solzhenitsyn took upon himself the singlehanded responsibility of exposing the truth of Stalin's reign of terror. He was convinced that if the facts could be recorded for the Russian people to read and understand, changes could ultimately be made in their lives. He wrote primarily for the benefit of his fellow Russians that they might come to see that changes are necessary in the Soviet penal system.

closed. In June, 1960 the first show trial of an Orthodox clergy-
man since 1927 took place. The defendant, the Archbishop of
Kazan, was sentenced to prison because he refused to cooperate
in the new crackdown.

For whatever reasons, Jewish religious practice was effectively
stifled almost to the extent that it had been under Stalin. The
Rabbinical Seminary, which had opened its doors in 1957 with
13 pupils, 11 of them over 40 years old, had its numbers reduced
to 4. The rationale for this drastic curtailment was the authorities'
refusal to permit some Asiatic students to return to Moscow on
the grounds that they had no residential permits in the capital.
Jewish theologians were prohibited from studying abroad or from
attending any international gathering of Jewish leaders. However,
the clergy of the Christian and Muslim faiths were granted such
privileges and the Russian Orthodox, Eastern Orthodox and
Protestant clergymen were allowed to join the World Council of
Churches.[8]

Khrushchev went a step beyond Stalin in restricting Jewish
institutions. In March, 1962, an order was issued outlawing the
baking of unleavened bread for Passover, an order that was re-
peated in 1963. He also allowed a radio program to be aired on a
small Ukrainian station in which the Jewish religion's sacred doctrine of the Chosen People was perverted for public mockery.

> . . . taking Biblical and liturgical phrases out of their
> religious context, the broadcaster denounced the Jews
> for aspiring to world domination, that good old anti-
> Semitic shibboleth, made doubly popular by the Nazi
> propaganda.[9]

Khrushchev also instituted charges of "espionage" against members of the two largest Jewish religious communities of Moscow
and Leningrad and many lay leaders were sentenced to long
prison terms for espionage.

The government also attacked Jewish ritual circumcision as
a "barbaric custom and a danger to health."[10]

---

[8]M. Decter, *Foreign Affairs*, XLI, 424ff.
[9]Baron, *The Russian Jew*, p. 342.
[10]*The New York Times*, December 20, 1959.

Before Khrushchev's crackdown, Jewish cultural life had preserved at least a modicum of dignity and creativity. In Yiddish culture between 1959-60 reprints of the works of Sholem Aleichem, Mendele and Peretz appeared and a single new volume was published to commemorate the 25th anniversary of Biro-Bidzhan. At the end of 1961, a new Yiddish literary journal, *Das Sovietishe Heimland,* commenced publication under the editorship of Aaron Vergelis who became the chief apologist for the Soviet treatment of Jews and speaking even in the United States in defense of the Soviet government.

One of the most frequent arguments advanced by Soviet officials in defending the diminution of Hebrew and Yiddish culture was that the Jews no longer cared for Hebrew and Yiddish letters.[11]

Understandably, one of the most notorious centers of anti-Semitism during Khrushchev's rule was the Ukraine. Since Khrushchev had taken a lenient stand on anti-Semitism in the Ukraine both before and after his rise to power, the Ukrainians were encouraged to perpetrate their anti-Semitic excesses. In 1963 the Ukrainian Academy of Science, the highest and most respected intellectual body in the Soviet Union, published a book by Trofim Kitchko, professor of philosophy and an ardent Ukrainian nationalist entitled *Judaism Without Embellishment.* The book was worthy of the hate literature produced in Hitler's Germany and made efficient use of the free hand Kitchko had been given to assail the ethics of the Bible and post-biblical Judaism. Although the book was denounced from all parts of the world and the Soviet government suffered some embarrassment from it in the light of their avowed policy of considering anti-Semitism a criminal act, Kitchko was not tried for a criminal act nor were his works suppressed.

The Soviet economy continued to make steady progress after the Second World War and consumer goods became more readily available, especially in the larger cities. But there were still shortages, poor quality merchandise, and other problems. Such

---

[11]Baron, *The Russian Jew,* p. 344.

conditions give impetus to black markets, currency speculation, and other prohibited practices.

> Since many Jews, especially in the older communities, still engaged in some form or other of merchandising, it was easy enough to place the blame on them as the economic criminals mainly responsible for these short-comings in the Soviet economy. Such economic subversion was now placed among the capital crimes because of its long-range counterrevolutionary effects. While there also were many non-Jewish economic criminals, in all public announcements Jews were singled out with great frequency. Even the numerous culprits who had Russianized their names were cited with their Jewish names in parentheses, so that no reader or broadcast listener could mistake their ethnic identity.[12]

According to reliable computation, among the 163 "economic criminals" condemned to death in 81 trials in 48 different cities between July 1961 and August 1963, no less than 88 and possibly 96, that is 50-60 percent, were easily identified as Jewish.[13] Economic crime legislation was utilized as a political weapon against Jews, priests, and medium-rank party officials. One outstanding example was the arrest of Olga Ivinskaia, a close friend of Boris Pasternak (within a few weeks of the latter's death) for an economic crime.

There has also been widespread discrimination against the admission of Jews to higher institutions of learning.

> Without facing the old formal numerus clausus, Jews, as a rule, had to be more gifted and more industrious in order to be chosen ahead of non-Jewish application.[14]

The author has heard numerous confirmations of this government-sanctioned discrimination from Russian Jews who had experienced it first hand.

---

[12]Ibid., p. 334.
[13]*Ibid.*
[14]*Ibid.*

Khrushchev's rule established the theoretical equality of the Jews in Soviet society and did away with the blatant terror and anti-Semitism of the Stalin era, perhaps paving the way for the growing opposition among the younger intelligentsia to anti-Semitism in any form. Yevgeny Yevtushenko's poem, *Babi Yar*, which describes the diabolical massacre in Kiev, was enthusiastically lauded in literary circles and in the numerous clubs where it was recited. But the poem certainly aroused the anger of Khrushchev and his government. When, "partly in protest against these governmental restrictions, partly as a repudiation of anti-Semitism, and partly out of idolization of the young poet, thousands of young Muscovites foregathered to listen to Yevtushenko's recitation of this poem in Moscow's Mayakovskii Square on Poets' Day of 1961"[15] they were dispersed by the police, carried away in vans 20 miles out of town and dumped on distant roads. Many of them returned the following day to demonstrate again and the police handled them roughly again. The prominent composer Dmitrii Shoshtakovich included *Babi Yar* along with 4 other poems in his Thirteenth Symphony, and Khrushchev reacted violently, suspending Shostakovich from any further performances after the second concert. At that point the poet and the composer yielded and inserted two lines in the composition: "I am proud of the Russia which stood in the path of (Nazi bandits)," and "Here together with Russians and Ukrainians lie Jews."

In spite of the power of a basically anti-Semitic government to force these two artists to submit to a dilution of their statement against the horrors visited upon the Jews, the poet and the composer are to be admired for their courage and willingness to expose a truth and reveal a sense of good-will that lies within the Russian people.

---

[15]*Ibid.*, p. 336.

Chapter Seven

BREZHNEV AND THE JEWS

Betram D. Wolfe has facetiously formulated a "law of diminishing dictators"[1] to explain changes in the top Soviet leadership: Lenin was a commanding personality in all respects; Stalin was intellectually limited but all powerful; Khrushchev had much less power despite high visibility; Brezhnev "is not there at all." Although there is some truth in Wolfe's "law" Brezhnev is, of course, "there."

Leonid Brezhnev was born in 1906 in the small river port at Kamenskoe (today Kneprodzerzhinsk) near Ekaterinoslav. In 1927 he completed a course in engineering at a technical institute in Kursk. After 3 years as a land surveyor in Kursk and Sverdlovsk, he studied for a year at the Agricultural Institute in Moscow and became a Party member. He served in the army for 2 years and in 1938 he became a full time Party worker and official in his home town, being promoted a year later to First Secretary of the region. During the Second World War, he served his country as a high political officer. After the war he served in Chernovtsy, Dnieper Area, and from 1950 to 1952 in Mododvia. From there he was recalled to Moscow and became a member of the Central Committee. Apparently attaching his fortunes to Khrushchev's, he became the latter's viceroy in Kazakhstan (1954-1956) and assumed important responsibilities for the development of a scheme for the cultivation of the virgin lands. In 1956 he returned to Moscow and became a candidate member of the presidium. In June, 1957 he became a full member. In May 1960 he became the President of the U.S.S.R. and remained in that position until 1964, when Mikoyan took over that position.

It is difficult to ascertain exactly how Brezhnev emerged as

---

[1]Donald W. Treadgold, *Twentieth Century Russia* (Chicago, 1972), p. 484.

senior leader when Khrushchev was demoted. His contributions to Marxist-Leninist theory were imperceptible and his political and economic skills were not manifested in any particular field.

With Khrushchev's dismissal, the office of Chairman of the Council of Ministers and that of first secretary of the Party were separated. Brezhnev became the first secretary and Kosygin (born in 1904) became the new chairman of the Council of Ministers. Thus Brezhnev and Kosygin shared a collective leadership.

The new leadership relaxed restrictions on the ownership of private plots and private livestock holdings, raised agricultural prices, and in general signaled a clear departure from Khrushchev's previously enunciated agricultural policies. This de-Stalinization process continued until 1965 when, in October, the long-standing proposals of Evsei Liberman, a Jewish professor at Kharkov University, were finally implemented in the area of economic reform. Liberman's proposals, which had been tried out in 1964 in two clothing factories at Bolshevichka and Maiak with initially favorable results, called for individual enterprises to be empowered to plan and produce in a way related to sales contracts with profits based on evaluation of performance.

By 1966 the Brezhnev regime embarked upon a two-pronged domestic policy: modest economic reform and limited crackdown on intellectual dissidence. The adoption of a harder line on the cultural front attracted the most attention abroad, almost all of it unfavorable.

In the field of religion, Brezhnev permitted the re-opening of about 500 churches out of 10,000 or so that had been closed during the previous 5 years. He also acceded in some minor respects to petitions from the Evangelical Christians and others for clarification of laws on religion and the conformity of practice with the law. However, in 1966-1967 a sharp crackdown on proselytization by the Baptists and Evangelists took place.

The plight of Soviet Jewry had deteriorated steadily though not spectacularly under Brezhnev. Concerned for their image in the eyes of the world, Brezhnev and his colleagues in the Kremlin have denied charges of anti-Semitism, but the incontrovertible facts speak for themselves.

Judaism in Soviet Russia has no organizational structure, and contact is not permitted between the various Jewish communities. On the other hand, the Russian Orthodox Church, the Georgian Orthodox Church, Islam and Buddhism all have central coordinating bodies which are legally authorized to convene congresses and conferences of their clergy and representatives of their adherents. Throughout the Soviet Union Jews are forbidden to issue even a single religious publication. The Russian Orthodox Church has an official publication which is issued by the highest authority in the hierarchy of that church. It also publishes religious works. The same applies to Islam. Yet no edition of the Bible in Hebrew has been published since 1917. The Bible in Russian, the original edition of which was published in 1926 for the benefit of the Russian Orthodox Church, was reprinted in 1957. Another Russian-Language Bible was issued specifically for the Baptists. The Koran was published for the Muslims in 1958. Jewish religious calendars are non-existent, yet each of the other major religions is supplied regularly by the legal central establishment of its faith. The last edition of the Jewish Prayer Book appeared in 1958, with only 3,000 copies. Each of the other religions is supplied with an adequate number of Prayer Books. No state aid is forthcoming for Judaism, yet the government places the publishing houses at the disposal of other religions and provides paper and other subsidies for publication. The production of prayer shawls, phylacteries and other religious items is in fact if not in principle forbidden for Jews. On the other hand, other faiths are permitted to produce the entire range of ritual objects—candles, crucifixes, rosaries, etc. Jews are prohibited from having contacts with organizations abroad. At the same time, Soviet Muslim students attend the El-Azhar religious university in Cairo, and Baptists study in Britain. The Russian Orthodox Church is affiliated with the Ecumencial Council of Churches and has sent observers to its Synod.

In 1969 Brezhnev's regime began to display more attention to some, but not all, Jewish religious needs. After many years of obstructing the baking of matzot for Passover, and after prohibiting it altogether in 1962—an act which provoked Jewish protests

BREZHNEV AND THE JEWS

throughout the world—the Soviet government removed these strictures before Passover, 1969. This marked the first time in many years that religious Jews in the Soviet Union under Brezhnev were able to observe Passover in a traditional manner.

Soviet officialdom has recently indicated that they may permit one young Jew to study for the rabbinate at a Rabbinical Seminary in Hungary. After his ordination he would return to Moscow as an ordained rabbi. Today more than 90 percent of the synagogues in the Soviet Union have no rabbis since no Yeshivot exist in the Soviet Union. The very few rabbis who are still alive are all over seventy. It would seem that allowing one young man to study for the rabbinate is nothing more than a token gesture with little meaning and little risk to the government.

The first national conference of Jewish religious leaders in the Soviet Union was held in March 1971, more than 53 years after the Bolshevik Revolution. Some 60 leaders of Jewish congregations from all parts of the Soviet Union gathered in Moscow and met for 6 hours in the Choral Synagogue, there to denounce Zionism and the State of Israel—without once mentioning any problems of Jewish life in the Soviet Union. It would seem that the conference was arranged by the Soviet authorities to counteract Jewish protests from abroad against anti-Jewish discrimination in the Soviet Union and the demand for free emigration of Jews from the U.S.S.R. to Israel voiced a a month earlier at the World Conference of Jewish Communities on Soviet Jewry in Brussels.

In the cultural sphere, despite the constantly brandished Yiddish monthly, *Sovietish Heimland,* and despite limited editions of a few works by deceased Yiddish authors, no Jewish self-expression worthy of the name has been authorized. Brezhnev and his government permit not even one single Jewish school, nor do they allow education in Hebrew, Yiddish or even in Russian about Judaism. No permanent Jewish theater exists. Almost everything that is published on Judaism is slanderous. To claim, as the Kremlin does, that the Soviet Jews have no interest whatsoever in their own culture and have freely chosen to assimilate into Russian culture is a flagrant distortion of the truth.

One of the greatest demands of Russian Jewry is for the Jewish theater and Yiddish concerts. Concerts by Jewish singers have been given from time to time in Moscow, Leningrad and other large cities, and they have filled the largest halls to capacity. Jewish songs are so popular in the Soviet Union that some Soviet singers include them in their concert repertoire. American singers like Jan Peerce and Paul Robeson, when giving concerts in Moscow, always include a few Jewish songs, to the delight of the audience which greets them with long-lasting enthusiastic applause. At such concerts one can feel that, assimilated or not, the Jewish spirit is still strongly alive among Jews in Russia.

In 1969, when no diplomatic relations existed between the Soviet Union and Israel, Nechama Lifshitz, the heart and soul of Jewish song in Russia, was permitted to emigrate to Israel. Under normal circumstance this might have been seen as a gesture of goodwill toward Jews. Sadly, at a time when the revival of Jewish culture in the Soviet Union needs such talents as Mrs. Lifshitz, her departure can only be interpreted as tragic proof that even she, whom the Soviet authorities always mentioned as evidence that there was no suppression of Jewish culture in Russia, had good grounds to seek emigration.

Schools of higher learning in the Soviet Union carry exact data on the numbers of their Jewish students. The information seems to appear with greatest ease when needed to convince one that no discrimination against Jews exists. There is no doubt that the government uses the information about a student's nationality to curtail Jewish ambitions for higher education and to encourage a larger proportion of non-Jews to enter universities. This fact is especially evident in the Ukraine, Byelorussia and the other Soviet Republics where nationalism is strong and where the non-Jewish population is comparatively less educated on the average than the Jewish.

However, the Soviet Union, with its expanding industry and technology, can hardly afford to discriminate against anyone who is a potential asset to the industrial development of the country or to its military machine. Thus Jews are now playing an important role as engineers in factories and in mines, in shipbuilding, and in the production of nuclear weapons, in sending satellites

to the moon, and in all branches of atomic science. Jews are also
quite active in the field of medicine, both as practicing physicians
and in medical research. Jews have a better chance in the fields
of higher mathematics, engineering and medicine than in other
fields, primarily because their country needs as many individuals
as possible in these fields.

In other fields of study the story is different. A young Jew,
for example, who has been teaching Russian literature at Moscow University describes how life can be for an intellectual who
is not engaged in the hard sciences:

> "I have been on the university's teaching staff for more
> than five years," he said. "But I do not think that I have
> a chance to reach a professorship soon, or even to be-
> come an assistant professor. It is more than four years
> since I submitted my doctoral thesis, but I have not been
> summoned as yet to defend it. Thus, I have not even re-
> ceived my doctorate, and who knews when I will ever
> receive it. My submitted thesis lies in a drawer some-
> where and is not being moved. In the meantime, I am
> teaching my subject as an instructor."[2]

He is certain that, were he not a Jew, he would have received
his doctorate long ago and would be well on his way to a professorship. "There is no hurry in the Soviet Union today to give the
professorship title to a Jew, unless he distinguishes himself in
atomic science," he reports.

In seeking to impress one with the argument that no anti-
Jewish bias is applied in schools of higher learning, Soviet officials
also point to the fact that the number of Jews engaged in research
work is increasing rather than decreasing every year. The estimate is that more than 50,000 Jews are now doing research work
in various fields. Authorities point out that the number of Ukrainians engaged in research work is only about 70,000 at a time when
there are 13 times as many Ukrainians in the Soviet Union as
there are Jews. Here they prefer to omit the fact that at least ⅔

----

[2]Boris Smolar, *Soviet Jewry Today and Tomorrow* (New York, 1972), p. 75.

of the Ukrainians are village people whose education is very limited.

> The general impression one gets after talking with all parties involved is that Jewish students find their way into Soviet universities but the tendency of the authorities is to hold their number down wherever possible. The fact that Jewish students must state their nationality on their application for admission to schools of higher learning, as must students of all other nationalities, makes it easier for the university authorities to choose between admitting them or applicants of other nationalities with equal marks in entrance examinations.[3]

As matters now stand, no Jewish applicant is certain that he will be admitted even if he passes with higher marks than a non-Jewish applicant. A certain percentage of Jewish students will always be found in Soviet universities, but that percentage may gradually wither with every year "because of the official view that place must be made for youths who are leaving the rural localities where they were born and moving to cities to get a higher education."[4] One may ask whether this means outright discrimination against the Jewish population in the Soviet Union. Perhaps not, but it does mean that a covert restrictive quota for Jews exists in schools of higher education and will probably continue to exist as long as the word "Jew" on the applicant's registration form provides an easy means of excluding him.

Another burning issue for Jews in general and Soviet Jewry in particular is the mass emigration of Soviet Jewry to Israel. Soviet officials, when reminded that Prime Minister Alexei N. Kosygin stated during a press conference in Paris on December 3, 1966 that Soviet Jews who wished to join members of their families abroad were free to do so, point out that this is still the policy of the Soviet government. When reminded that this does not seem the case, judging from protest by Soviet Jews to the United Nations about their having been refused exit visas to join

---

[3]*Ibid.*, p. 76.
[4]*Ibid.*

their relatives in Israel, the officials try to evade the issue by answering that since Moscow does not maintain diplomatic relations with Israel at present, emigration is looked upon as an expression of taking the side of Israel in the Soviet-Israeli rift. When the Soviet officials are queried about the arrest and dismissal of Jewish applicants for emigration visas from their jobs, they deny it. However when they are confronted with names and verified cases, the authorities claim that the measures were taken because the applicants allegedly indulged in Zionist propaganda.

In an interview with Boris Smolar in 1968, one of the Soviet officials somewhat lifted the curtain hanging over the question of Jewish emigration from Soviet Russia.

> ". . . despite the fact that we consider the State of Israel an enemy, and notwithstanding the fact that we broke diplomatic relations with Israel in 1967, our authorities are still granting exit visas today to Jews who had applied for emigration to Israel before 1967. It is true that the number of such visas is small, but the very fact that we are still issuing them should serve as proof to you that we are not arresting Jews who apply for emigration."[5]

The unusual tension and the great relief which were felt by Soviet Jews in the wake of Israel's victory in the Six-Day War coincided with the first appearance of non-Jewish protest in the U.S.S.R. for human rights and for more national rights for minorities as well as with a strengthening of formal legalism and the relative easing of centralized control. The Soviet Union had also signed the Universal Declaration of Human Rights and ratified an international convention establishing, among other things, that every person has the right to leave every country, including his own. In this atmosphere began the wave of courageous demands by Soviet Jews, particularly the younger generation, for the right to leave the U.S.S.R. and emigrate to Israel, both within the framework of "family reunion" as in the past and as "repatriation" to the historical national homeland of the Jewish people.

---

[5]*Ibid.*, p. 174.

High Soviet officials in Moscow, when you mention the subject of Jewish emigration, give you the impression that the subject is very much on the mind in the Kremlin but is being held in abeyance for the time being. When the Arab-Israeli war is over and relations between the Soviet Union and Israel are reestablished, the Soviet Government may not be averse to permitting Jewish emigration to Israel on the basis of family reunification even though emigration is otherwise banned.[7]

It is important to analyze the events that prompted Brezhnev and other Kremlin leaders to change their policy towards Jewish emigration to Israel, irrespective of family reunification. The Leningrad Trials of 1970,[8] which were intended to instill fear in the hearts of the oppressed Jews and to crush the sudden renaissance of Jewish spirit, engendered monumental consequences, international in scope, that were detrimental to Soviet policy in awakening sympathy for Soviet Jews throughout the world. The Jewish national movement was enkindled like the "burning bush" to an extent "never contemplated, assuming forms of an escalating stubbornness and militancy that only a full-blown return to Stalinist terrorism—impossible under current Soviet circumstances —could have destroyed."[9] An international clamor initiated by world Jewry condemned Soviet actions. Even the Russian humanistic intelligentsia began to defend the Jewish activists.

One can conclude that the Leningrad Trials were a grave blunder by Brezhnev—a blunder with national as well as international ramifications. It led to exit visas for thousands of Jews to leave Russia, though they were also burdened with a host of arbitrarily imposed obstacles.

In addition, Soviet foreign policy played an important role in relaxing restrictions against Jewish emigrants to Israel. Under Brezhnev's leadership the government realized that a detente

---

[7]*Ibid.*, p. 185.

[8]For details of the Leningrad Trials see the excellent work of William Korey, *The Soviet Cage: Anti-Semitism in Russia* (New York: The Viking Press, 1973), pp. 201-276.

[9]*Ibid.*, p. xii.

with the United States and NATO would be highly advantageous
for her. It has attempted to defuse international tensions; stabilize
the status quo in Central and Eastern Europe; and establish trade
and commercial relations with the capitalist countries.[10] In particular, it has proved important for Russia to seek satisfactory relations with America in light of a thorny foreign policy with Red
China as that country began to achieve a mutual understanding
with the United States.

There is ample evidence that pressure by the United States
can remove some of the obstacles to obtaining emigration visas.
For example, the Jackson Amendment to the East-West Relations
Act submitted to the Senate by 76 senators specified that Congress would not approve a proposed Soviet-American trade agreement unless the "diploma tax" was dropped. It also stated that "no
nonmarket economy shall be eligible to receive most-favored nation treatment or to participate in any program of the government of the United States which extends credits or credit guar-
antees" if that country "imposes more than a nominal tax on
emigration, for any purposes or cause whatsoever."[11]

Despite Brezhnev's change in policy regarding emigration to
Israel, world Jewry and the free world cannot afford to relax their
demands for religious and cultural rights for Soviet Jewry at home
and for those who desire to relocate themselves to the land of their
fathers. Russia's policy can harden if she sees that a "non-involve-
ment policy" prevails regarding the Russian Jews. Silence was perhaps a cause of Hitler's success in destroying six million Jews and
the Bolsheviks' annihilation of religious and cultural life during
the Second World War. Vigilance, care, diplomacy, power and
pressure must be the guide for world Jewry as well as for all men
of good will in constantly reminding Soviet leaders that a Jew
should have equal rights at home and the privileges to emigrate
if he or she chooses to do so. Gone forever must be the days when
a Jew could be silently exiled to Siberia "for rehabilitation," as
was the case of the author's father and thousands of others. The

---

[10]*Ibid.*, p. 296.
[11]The text of Jackson's Amendment can be found in Korey, *The Soviet Cage,*
p. 319.

Jew in the free world must never forget that he is "his brother's keeper" and must remind non-Jews that every man is created in the image of God and is entitled to a life of freedom, dignity, and security.

CHAPTER EIGHT

COMMUNISM VERSUS ZIONISM

It is one of history's ironic twists of fate that the origins of two conflicting manifestations of nationalistic yearning—Russian Communism and Israel-oriented Zionism—occurred almost simultaneously. In 1917, the Bolshevik Revolution wrote an end to centuries of Tsarist repression and gave birth to the proletarian society of Soviet Communism. That same year, the promulgation of the Balfour Declaration spurred the hopes of Diaspora Jewry for the re-birth of a Jewish homeland in Palestine, the primary political purpose of the Zionist movement.

Communism and Zionism emerged together, only to clash at once. Although it appeared that the struggle between these political philosophies would be fought on ideological grounds, in reality the conflict emerged as a matter of pragmatic politics. Lenin saw Great Britain as epitomizing world capitalism, and Britain's encouragement of mass Russian Jewish emigration to Palestine motivated him to mount a campaign against Zionism. At the same time, such key leaders of the Zionist movement as Chaim Weizmann and Vladamir Jabotinsky theorized that to realize the Zionist dream they must join forces with the Western Powers combatting Communism.

In the early twenties, an emissary of the Zionist executive, Dr. Eder, did make an effort to foster coexistence between Communism and Zionism. He went to Moscow seeking to make the right connections through a fellow Jew, Maxim Litvinov, with whom he had been friendly during the latter's exile in London and who was later to become Soviet Foreign Minister. But Zionism had been so completely linked with the Balfour Declaration and the British Mandate in Palestine (a "tool of British imperialism") that Eder spent fruitless weeks in Moscow meeting no one.

73

Jews in Eastern Europe became ideologically torn between Zionism sentiment and Communist doctrine. From 1917 to 1920, a period of storm and stress, a fateful debate took place within the Poale Zion World Union. Vain attempts were made here as well to foster a reconciliation between Zionism and Communism. The decisive battle was joined in August, 1920, at the Poale Zion Conference in Vienna. Two camps had formed in this labor wing of the Zionist movement. The Rightist delegates from the Western Countries—North America, Western Europe, and Palestine— led by Ben-Gurion and Ben-Zvi, stressed Jewish settlement in Palestine as their supreme concern and called for mass immigration of Jews to Palestine. This group placed its political hopes with the British Mandate and the democratic parties who opposed the Soviet dictatorship.

The Leftist delegates from Russia, the Ukraine, Poland and the Central European countries followed the teachings of Borochov, founder of the Russian Poale Zion. Before his death in 1917 Borochov theoretically reconciled Zionism with Communism. He held that Zionism is a social movement and that the crucial contribution of Zionist Socialism to the Jewish renaissance was to claim that Zionism could never succeed as a purely political national movement, but would also have to be a movement of social revolution, aimed at reshaping the social composition of the Jewish people. Jews, the argument ran, are to be found primarily in the middle classes; they lack a well-rounded social structure; there are no Jewish peasants, no Jewish workers, very few Jewish artisans.

The Vienna Conference ended in a split between the two ideologies. The path taken by the Rightists led to the establishment of the State of Israel and that of the Leftists led to their ultimate dissolution, although for a time the leftist Poale Zion succeeded in functioning as a viable political force in Russia.

Ironically, Borochov's writings—which had inspired the leftist movement—were also the basis for Israeli Socialism as established by the Rightists.

> Hence the painful decision, not an easy one for Socialists
> to arrive at, to bar cheap Arab labor from Jewish settle-

ments, so as not to create a White-settler, colony-like European elite living off cheap "native labor." It surely is a paradox that it had been this insistence of the Zionist labor movement on "Jewish labor," which excluded the Arab agricultural proletariat from the Jewish labor market, which saved the Yishuv from the social fate of a South Africa or an Algeria; socially, economically and nationally, the idea of Zionism was exactly the opposite of the White-settler communities in the Third World.[1]

This action defied the economic forces of the market, supplanted cheap Arab labor with more expensive and less experienced Jewish labor and ultimately resulted in the deliberate creation of a Jewish peasantry and a Jewish working class, the most revolutionary downward mobility ever experienced in social history.

It was the same conceptual framework which placed the kibbutzim and moshavim in such socially strategic positions in Israeli society, created the Histadrut not as a mere trade union organization but as a Society of Laborers (Hevrat Ovdim), owning industries, banks and cooperatives and trying to coordinate a vision of social reconstruction with political aims and manipulation.[2]

In other words, Socialism and Zionism became inseparable. The socialistically oriented structure became pivotal to the establishment of a Jewish society.

In 1922 Wolf Averbach, the leader of the Russian Jewish Community Party, visited Palestine. He urged Russian Jewish youth to go to Palestine and transform the land of the Bible into a "dictatorship of the proletariat," which would in fact have been all-Jewish, since the Arabs were then still too immersed in Islam to experiment with Communism and its atheistic ideology. When Lenin and his followers frowned upon the Jewish Communist

[1]Shlomo Avineri, "Israel's Socialist Heritage," in *The Jewish Advocate*, April 2, 1970.
[2]*Ibid.*

Party they disbanded themselves, although a splinter group calling itself Left Poale Zion-C.D. continued to exist legally until the end of the decade, when Zionism was officially outlawed in the Soviet Union. Few, if any, of the Zionist Communists were to survive: they were disposed of by the Secret Police.

In neighboring Poland, the Jewish Communist Party, called Left Poale Zion, survived after a fashion. Though disowned by Moscow, it supported the Soviets and collaborated with the clandestine Polish Communist Party which included many non-Zionist Jews who despised the pro-Communist Zionists. At the same time, without belonging to the Zionist organization, the Left Poale Zion strongly supported the Zionist cause.

In Palestine itself, 46 years ago, the underground Palestine Communist Party met and very nearly broke up over the question of possible joint action between Zionism and Communism. The minority proclaimed an anathema on Zionism and advocated affiliation with the Communist Internationale. The majority yielded and, for more than 4 decades, the largely Jewish Palestinian Party scrupulously toed the anti-Zionist line of the world Communist movement.

Despite these minor attempts at accommodations, Communism and Zionism could never reconcile their basic philosophical differences. Only once in the half-century since the Balfour Declaration has Communism abated its hostility towards Zionism. After the Nazi massacre of six million Jews, including nearly two million Russian Jews, the Soviet Union joined the United States in pronouncing a blessing on the rebirth of the State of Israel. This was in 1947, when Gromyko delivered an historic address to the United Nations supporting Israel. Barzilai was later to write of this action:

> The Kremlin had its political motives. It wanted to secure a footing in the Middle East. French imperialism in the region had been evicted by British imperialism. And now the Jews of Eretz Yisrael were giving the British the push. So at that time the Zionists were looked upon by Moscow as acceptable allies—all the more acceptable since the Russians had tried and failed to reach an un-

derstanding with the Arab nationalists. . . . In the circumstances then prevailing, Moscow could do no better than back Israel.[3]

At this time Stalin was at the height of his power. He established diplomatic relations with Israel in 1948, instructing his diplomats to pursue a three-point plan: (1) to alienate Israel from the United States; (2) to undermine relations between the Jews in Israel and Jews in the free world; and (3) to organize an Israeli fifth column to collaborate with the Red Army which was to carry out an armored invasion over the mountains of Anatolia, across Syria and Israel to the banks of the Suez Canal.[4]

Ben-Gurion recognized Soviet plans and sought to resist Russian expansionism by turning to the West. In the last fifteen years, the struggle between Zionism and Communism has grown ever sharper. Moscow broke off diplomatic relations with Israel before Stalin's death and restored them after he was buried. But under Khrushchev and through the intermediary of Czechoslovakia the Soviets began to supply arms to Egypt. This ushered in a new era in Soviet relations with the Arab world.

By 1965, it became clear to Israel's Communists that there could no be compromise between the Soviets' extreme pro-Arab stand and the State of Israel. Israel's Communist Party consequently split into two factions. The one led by the Jew, Vilner, attracted all the Arab Communists in Israel and received 75 percent of Communist votes cast in the last parliamentary elections. The other, the all-Jewish nonconformist group, which claimed that Communism was compatible with Zionism, obtained the remaining 25 percent. During the Six-Day War, the Soviet-directed Arab aim was to annihilate Israel and its Jewish population. Israel victoriously foiled the attempt. Now a new round has opened in the more than 50-year-old duel between Communism and Zionism.

In February-March, 1970, the Soviet government issued a pamphlet on Soviet opinion about events in the Middle East and

---

[4]Y. Barzilai (known as Yosef Berger, founder of the Communist Party of Palestine, survivor of 22 years of Russian prisons and slave labor camps), "Communism V. Zionism, in *Israel Magazine*, Vol. 1, no. 3, May, 1968.
[4]*Ibid.*

the adventures of international Zionism entitled, *Zionism: Instrubent of Imperialist Reaction.* The pamphlet claims that:

> The Zionist conception of Israel is based, first and foremost, on aggression and territorial expansion. Catholic scholastics have long stopped claiming that an infinite number of angels can stand on the tip of a needle. Zionist theoreticians seem to realize, too, that no infinite number of immigrants can be settled in the vicinity of Mount Zion. And so, in the course of half a century, we have been witnessing the metamorphosis of initially modest Zionist claims about a "national hearth," proposed after the end of World War I by Lord Balfour, into the idea of a great empire which the present champions of the "Movement for Great Israel" are striving to set up.
>
> . . . in theory and practice Israeli Zionism is akin to imperialism. It is not surprising that Western imperialist powers support Tel Aviv, since they have similar ideological views and consider Israel an imperialist outpost in the Middle East.
>
> . . . Zionism, like any other reactionary ideology, is an ideology of exploiters; it resorts to slander campaigns and hypocritical propaganda stunts. Thus, the real tragedy of the Jews in countries which were under the Nazi yoke is being used to camouflage the neo-fascist practice of today's Israel.[5]

In light of such statements and the Yom Kippur War, Zionism and the State of Israel will be confronted with the arduous task of achieving harmony with Soviet Communism. However, let us not fear if contradictions in theory remain so long as a peaceful co-existence between Israel and Russia can prevail in practice. Theoretical differences do not kill people and start wars. It is real events, such as supplying the latest weapons, that create an atmosphere for war. Let us hope that Zionism and Communism can coexist peacefully through mutual understanding of each other's ideologies.

---

[5]*Zionism: Instrument of Imperialist Reaction* (Moscow: Novosti Press Agency Publishing House, 1970), p. 62.

CHAPTER NINE

SOVIET FOREIGN POLICY IN THE MIDDLE EAST

Soviet Russia's involvement in the Middle East traces its roots to the foreign policy of the Tsars. Catherine the Great (1762-1795), Nicholas I (1825-1855) and Alexander II (1855-1881) all envisioned the acquisition of warm-water ports to the south.

In an 1953 article in the *Herald Tribune* Karl Marx warned Western powers about Tsarist Russia's expansionist policy in the Middle East. Little did Marx know that in 1917 Russia would become the first country to establish a government based on Communism; and that in the 1960s she would be firmly entrenched in the Middle East.

Although the Tsars themselves failed in their attempts to gain a stronghold in the Middle East, their aim has been ardently pursued by Communist leaders in this century.

1948-1953

In official Communist eyes, the Middle East and North Africa represented targets of the "anti-colonial type" in the world struggle against capitalism. One Marxist-Leninist theory regarding the struggle against capitalism in the underdeveloped countries prophesied that if the capitalists were deprived of their source of raw materials and of their markets in these areas, their economic system would weaken and inevitably collapse.[1] In 1924 Stalin presented his view on the anti-colonial struggle in a lecture in Moscow:

Formerly it was tacitly assumed that the victory of the proletariat in Europe was possible without a direct alliance with the movement for emancipation in the col-

---

[1] J. M. Mackintosh, *Strategy and Tactics of Soviet Foreign Policy* (New York, 1963), p. 117.

79

onies. Leninism has proved that the road to victory in the
West lies through a revolutionary alliance with the lib-
eration movement of the colonies and dependent terri-
tories. This does not mean that the proletariat must support every national movement. Cases occur when national movements in certain oppressed countries come
into conflict with the interests of the proletarian movement. In such cases, support is, of course, entirely out
of question. For national movements must be examined
concretely from the point of view of the interests of the
revolutionary movement and not from the point of view
of abstract rights.[2]

This statement accurately portrays Stalin's foreign policy towards the Middle East throughout his lifetime. In 1945-1946, the
Soviet government had made an abortive attempt to use its forces
stationed in Northern Persia to detach a province from the Per-
sian State. Because of its failure, Stalin decided to use propaganda rather than force against the established governments and
their alliances. Each of the Middle Eastern governments, including the anti Western government of Dr. Mossadeq of Persia,[3] was
bitterly attacked in this way. On April 29, 1950, the Soviet army
paper, *Red Star,* portrayed the Arab League as

> . . . an instrument for the enslavement of the peoples
> of the Arab East by the British imperialists. The British
> and American imperialists are jointly exploiting the
> League's leaders, who are obedient to them, for the re-
> alization of a further war and the suppression of the
> progressive forces of the countries of the Middle East.

After the Second World War, Soviet Russia's foreign policy
in the Middle East was based on the logic of what was best for
the Soviet Union, and that was primarily to dislodge Great Britain
from the area.

---

[2]*Ibid.,* p. 117.

[3]By the Azerbaijan "Democratic" Radio on Soviet territory in the Caucasus on
January 30, 1952. See Mackintosh, *Strategy and Tactics of Soviet Foreign Policy,*
p. 118.

The Soviet government decided to support the establishment of a Jewish State in Palestine because it afforded an opportunity to reduce Great Britain's influence in the area and to establish a Russian base in Israel during the Cold War. For years, the Communists had castigated Zionism as a wicked bourgeois concept and a tool of British imperialism. But in 1947-48, Andrei Gromyko delivered impassioned speeches for the formation of a Jewish State, appealing to the conscience of mankind. "During the last war, the Jewish people underwent indescribable sorrow and suffering," Gromyko reminded UN delegates. "No Western European State was able to help the Jewish people to defend its rights and its very existence. Now thousands are still behind barbed wire. . . . The time has come to help these people not by words but by deeds.[4] This diplomacy, together with the military aid of the Soviet Union and the Communist bloc, played a significant role in the establishment of the State of Israel and in the defeat of the Arabs in the War of Independence.

Diplomatic representatives of the United States and the Soviet Union were the first to come to Israel, arriving within a few days of each other, early in August, 1948. In a Tel Aviv hotel packed to the rafters, they found lodging under the same roof. The hotel erected two flagstaffs, from which the Stars and Stripes and the Hammer and Sickle fluttered side by side. Beset by Arab armies, the Israelis could lean confidently upon the shoulders of the two mightiest nations on earth. More than this, there prevailed a feeling that Israel somehow brought East and West together. If the two great superpowers could act in harmony, at least on Israel, why should they not come to agree on other things? The Messianism latent in the Jewish soul, stimulated by the rebirth of the Jewish State, was ready to embrace the entire world. With the fulfillment of the Biblical prophecy, a new era of peace and good-will could be dawning for all men.

David Ben-Gurion, in a statement issued after the General Assembly's resolution of November 29, 1947, expressed this idea very guardedly:

The cooperation of America and Russia in a solution of

---

[4]Lester Velie, *Countdown in the Holy Land* (Min.) 1969), pp. 24f.

the Palestine problem is bound to serve as an encouragement to all those who, in common with the Jewish people, believe in the possibility of permanent co-operation
between East and West for the furtherance of permanent
peace in the world.[5]

1953-1967

Early in the 1950s in most Arab countries, the Communist
Party was either outlawed or just in its infancy. Immediately before the death of Stalin, however, Communists like Khalid Bik-
dash, the Syrian Communist Party leader, appeared as candidates
in parliamentary elections, and Communist propaganda promul-
gated the needs for "broad popular fronts uniting all national
forces."

Premier Malenkov, in his speech of August 8, 1953 to the Supreme Soviet, made the earliest friendly gestures to the established Middle Eastern governments, as well as to those of India
and South-East Asia. At the end of the year, Cairo began to make
favorable references to Soviet Foreign policy, and to use the word
"neutrality" as a possible foreign policy for countries like Egypt.
Early in 1954, Egypt carried out a number of barter agreements
with Eastern European countries for the purchase of cotton, the
sale of which is so necessary for her economy. In September, 1954
the Soviet government opened a cultural center in Cairo. Thus,
before Malenkov's loss of power in the Soviet Union, the first steps
had been taken by the Soviets to formulate "a policy of economic
and political penetration of the Arab countries in the Middle
East."[6]

Khrushchev's decision to sell arms to Egypt and Syria was
prompted by the Baghdad Pact, the creation of military alliance
between states near the Soviet frontier, with the additional support of Great Britain, a world power and a signatory of NATO.
The Baghdad Pact was regarded by the Soviet government as a
potential military threat to its security. While it may be argued

---

[5]See Ben-Gurion's Statement in Walter Eytan, *The First Ten Years* (New
York, 1958), p. 139.
[6]Mackintosh, *Strategy and Tactics of Soviet Foreign Policy*, p. 119.

that the Pact was purely defensive and that the armed forces of its members—Iraq, Turkey, Pakistan, Great Britain and Iran— were no threat to the mighty Soviet Union, this reasoning would be regarded as fallacious by Soviet strategists. According to Soviet analysis, the creation of even the weakest Western military pact does two things: first, it makes it legally possible for the strong powers of the West, at some stage in the future, to find excuses for the establishment of up-to-date offensive bases, perhaps with nuclear and rocket capability, in the vicinity of the alliance. Secondly, by committing at least one major power to the defense of nations along the Soviet border so that an attack on one of them might lead to the outbreak of a global conflict, it restricts and limits the freedom of action of the Soviet Union in dealing with its neighbors.

In the case of the Baghdad Pact, Soviet Russia was confronted with

> a dilemma in planning its reaction to the alliance. Nikita Khrushchev decided upon the sale of weapons to Egypt. This was a political reaction by limited military means designed to raise Egyptian prestige and build Egypt up as the focal point for Arab loyalties, and consequently to lower Iraq's position in the Arab world. Khrushchev's decision was, in fact, in the nature of an emergency measure, superimposed on the existing strategy because of Western initiatives in the Middle East, but was not intended to replace the longer-term economic and political campaign to drive Western influence out of the Middle East.[7]

It so happened that Colonel Nasser of Egypt also disliked the Baghdad Pact for reasons of his own. He stood for "active neutralism," that is, he wanted the Western Powers to keep out of the Middle East, so he himself would be the dominant figure in the area. Furthermore, he was annoyed to see Iraq, Egypt's traditional rival in the Arab world, enjoying pre-eminence in the

---

[7] See Binyamin Eliav (a former political advisor to Golda Meir), "Russian Drive in the Middle East," in *Israel Magazine*, Vol. I, no. 3, May, 1968.

new Western-inspired Middle East set up. So he turned to the Russians who were glad to supply him with what he wanted most, a huge arsenal "to brandish, not against the Baghdad Pact nations who were too big to be intimidated, but against Israel." Thus Nasser finally asserted himself as the true leader of Pan-Arabism against the intruder, Israel.[8]

The then Israeli Prime Minister Moshe Sharett hastened to Geneva to express deep concern to Soviet Foreign Minister Molotov, who reportedly answered: "Don't worry, you won't hurt. There'll be no Arab-Israeli War. The Great Powers won't stand for it. It might jeopardize world peace."[9] Molotov was quite possibly sincere. But the Soviet government had created a situation that was bound to lead to an explosion. Emboldened by his stock of Russian weapons, Nasser ordered a series of fedayin terrorist incursions into Israel, which culminated in the massacre of school children in the Habad Village near Tel Aviv. In 1956, the Sinai War erupted in full force.

Khrushchev and Kremlin authorities, for their part,

> after obtaining a foothold in the Middle East, grew increasingly acquisitive. The momentum of their penetration stemmed also from nervousness. Arab governments are liable to chop and change. Therefore Russia must all the time enlarge her—mainly military—aid and make the Egyptians and other Arabs increasingly dependent on Moscow. Russia can afford to be generous with weapons, which become quickly obsolete as between one Superpower and another, but which are still ultra-modern in the armies of smaller nations and are the most coveted commodity of petty dictatorships like Egypt, Syria and Iraq.[10]

Israel's victory in the Six-Day War prompted Moscow's immediate decision in June 1967 to speedily restore the shattered balance of power in the Middle East by a massive air-lift of modern arms to Egypt and Syria and by an unprecedented diplomatic and

[8]Ibid.
[9]Ibid.
[10]Ibid.

propaganda barrage to force Israel to withdraw unconditionally to the pre-war lines. The reasons for such a decision lie in Russia's ambition to remain a superpower, to check America's strategy of global supremacy, and to appease the "hawks" in her politburo. The Westernizing "dove," who preferred to give first priority not to Russia's ambition abroad, but to the modernization of her own economy and society, regarded the frantic pro-Arab, anti-Israel drive as an unpleasant necessity in order to avoid the sudden crumbling of Russia's international position. With the "hawks" it was different. It was their dream that Russia's empire should embrace a Soviet-Arab bloc with Egypt, Syria, Yemen, Algeria and Iraq as likely members for a start.[11]

By 1968, Egypt, Algeria, Syria and Iraq had received a total of more than three billion dollars in Soviet military aid, including over 3,500 tanks, 900 modern warplanes and uncounted masses of artillery. Egypt has been the main beneficiary of this generosity. Half the tanks and 700 of the planes went to Egypt. With Soviet aid alone, the Egyptian navy has become—on paper at least—one of the five most powerful in the world. It includes 7 destroyers, 12 submarines, 18 Komar and Ossam missile-vessels, 12 anti-submarine boats and 30 torpedo boats. American intelligence sources estimate that by 1968 the Soviet Union had replaced about one-half of the aircraft and armor that Egypt lost during the Six-Day War. The Israeli estimate is much higher. There is a general consensus that in the two months following the war 250 flights of giant Soviet Antonov cargo planes airlifted nearly 200 warplanes and 250 tanks into Egypt; and that in the following two months, Soviet ships brought in 140 tanks and 40 to 50 planes.[12]

In 1968 Western intelligence sources reported that for the first time technicians, advisors, and instructors had penetrated as deep as the battalion formations of the Egyptian army and Soviet military doctrine was being taught even on the tactical level.

By far the most dramatic development since the June war and, indeed, in the entire course of the Soviet Union's increasing involvement in the Middle East, "is provided by the birth of the

---

[11]*Ibid.*
[12]Michael Elkins (correspondent in Israel for B.B.C. and CBS), "The Warm Water Bear," in *Israel Magazine*, Vol. I, no. 3, May, 1968.

Russian Navy's Mediterranean squadron—sometimes called 'the Soviet Shest (or Sixth) Fleet.' "[13]

On July 10, 1968, units of the Soviet Navy arrived at Port Said and Alexandria for a "courtesy visit." They included one cruiser, one destroyer, two submarines, two guided-missile carriers, five landing craft, and an oil tanker. They were commanded by Admiral Igor Molochov who promptly announced that his force was "prepared to cooperate with the Egyptian armed forces to repel any aggression."

At the time, Western governments interpreted the presence of the Soviet ships and Admiral Molochov's statement as being aimed at Israel. But the "courtesy visit" has been indefinitely extended; the number of "guests" has been increased by another cruiser, two more missile-equipped destroyers, six submarines, a floating dock to service the fleet, and an "ice-breaker" which is widely believed to be an electronic intelligence ship since there has not been ice in the Mediterranean within recorded history.

Western observers have been compelled to revise their original estimate that the Soviet Navy had ventured into the Mediterranean merely to offer temporary security to the beaten Egyptians —or to erase from Arab minds the memory of Russia's ineffective support during the June war. According to the outgoing commander-in-Chief of the American Sixth Fleet, Admiral John S. McCain, Jr., Soviet naval presence in the Mediterranean increased ten fold between 1963 and 1966. United States Navy sources estimate that Soviet naval operating days in the Mediterranean (the number of ships multiplied by the number of their sailings days) was 400 percent greater in 1967 than in 1963; the relevant figure for Soviet submarines is up 2,000 percent.

It is a fact that the Soviet Union is the second largest naval power in the world and is capable of a vast build-up in a selected area on relatively short notice. The first basic requirement of Soviet military and geopolitical strategy in the Middle East has already been achieved and even surpassed—the area is no longer a Western bastion, the Mediterranean is no longer the *mare nostrum* of the Western powers.

---

[13]*Ibid.*

While this has been happening, not only is the Baghdad Pact long dead, but CENTO (Central Treaty Organization of Great Britain, Pakistan, Iran and Turkey, with the United States outside but supplying the funds and equipment) has been undermined. In 1972 Sadat suddenly announced the withdrawal of Russian personnel from Egypt. Yes, Russia withdrew some men but no one can ascertain whether all or only some of the advisors left Egypt. Furthermore, one must remember that Russian naval power still remains firmly entrenched in the waters of the Middle East.

For Israelis and Jews the world over, the peace and prayer of their holiest day, Yom Kippur, was tragically shattered when the Arabs launched an attack against Israel on October 6, 1973. For the Arabs it was a holy season, too, the month-long fast of Ramadan, which many of the Muslim's associate with the greatest glories of their past. Both sides accuse each other of starting the unexpected war. However, there is ample evidence, both from the United Nations observers on the scene and from the actual course of battle that "suggests that the Arabs struck first, in a deliberate campaign carefully coordinated between Egypt and Syria."[14]

It is of importance to analyze the role of the Soviet Union in this costly and tragic war. The supplies provided in advance to the Egyptian, Syrian and Iraqi governments convinced the Arabs that they could start the fourth round in the last 25 years. Among the three armies named, the Soviet leaders supplied close to 6,000 new tanks. The models delivered have been the newest and finest Soviet tanks, the T-62, plus large additional numbers of the preceding model, the T-55.[15] The T-62 is the newest tank in the Soviet armored forces. The Soviet Union delivered to the Arab armies "almost limitless numbers of the most advanced Soviet anti-aircraft missiles, the Sam-2 improved, the Sam-3, and the particularly troublesome Sam-6."[16] The missiles were supplied before the attack and these were supplemented by thousands of the Soviet's portable, bazooka-like aircraft killer for infantry units, the Grail.

---

[14]The New York Times, October 8, 1973.
[15]The Washington Post, October 19, 1973.
[16]Ibid.

The Soviet's aid program also included a series of anti-tank missiles. The main ones were the "RPG-7, already unhappily met by our own forces against the North Vietnamese, and the two highly efficient wire-guided tank killers, the Sapper and the Sagger."[17] One of the latter killed the Israeli tank commander in the Sinai, Brig. Gen. Albert Mendler.

The question can now be raised as to whether the Russians had any foreknowledge of the Arab attack on Israel. It is crystal clear that the Soviet leaders had foreknowledge of the immediate treacherous war and they did nothing to deter it. Two days before war broke out they did remove some of their personnel from Egypt and Syria as a token of disapproval. As bitter fighting erupted on both fronts, key Soviet technicians in Egypt and fair numbers of important military admisors in Syria remained to aid in the Arab war effort against Israel.

Leonid Brezhnev wrote personal letters to King Hussein of Jordan, King Hassan of Morocco and Habib Bourbuiba of Tunisia to send troops to the Syrian and Egyptian fronts.[18] In addition, there were huge resupplies airlifted. Between 75 and 100 sorties of the big Soviet transports, the Antanov 12 and Antanov 22 have reached Syria and Egypt. Tanks and other armored vehicles are also being landed in the ports of Alexandria and Latakiah.[19]

In the realm of anti-Israel propaganda in the United Nations and in the world, Russian leaders have called Israel "barbaric" and Jacob Malik walked out on Yosef Tekoah's presentation in the Security Council. It appears that in the eyes of mother Russia, her children, the Arabs, are always innocent, and that aggressor Israel is always the culprit. Subjectivity and love are endearing qualities, but they do not necessarily represent the true facts so essential for fairness and objectivity.

As long as the Syrians and the Egyptians were on the offensive and inflicting heavy casualties upon the Israelis, the Soviet Union refrained from calling for a cease-fire. However, as soon as it became apparent that Israel had assumed the offensive, the Kremlin leadership urged America to pressure Israel to agree to an imme-

---

[17]*Ibid.*
[18]*The New York Times,* October 10, 1973.
[19]*The Washington Post,* October 19, 1973.

diate cease-fire. Russia realized that General Ariel (Arik) Sharon's breakthrough to the west bank of the Suez Canal in a bid to win a quick, decisive victory would be detrimental to Egypt as well as to her own interests. When 20,000 soldiers of the Egyptian III Corps were trapped and cut off from supplies, Russia called for an immediate cease-fire.[20] Israel was pressured to allow the encircled Egyptian III Corps to be resupplied by truck convoy, a situation unparalleled in modern military history. "The agreement came, according to well-placed official sources, after the United States told the Israeli Government Friday night that the Soviet Union had threatened to save the Egyptian force, which is surrounded on the east bank of the Suez Canal."[21]

One can question whether the Russians meant to carry out their threat. But there is positive evidence that when America put its forces around the world on the alert Russia backed down. Power and might are very effective weapons that the Soviet Union respects and fears. Thus, one can conclude that Russia's intention to intervene militarily to save the III Corps was real. Furthermore, it shows the extent of Soviet involvement in the Middle East and its desire to remain as an active participant, supplier of weaponry, advisor, and arbiter of the destiny of the inhabitants of the region.

America and the world must take heed that peace between the Arabs and the Israelis also depends upon catering to the whims and understanding the machiavellian machinations and ulterior motives of Soviet foreign policy in the Middle East. Strength and power, as displayed by President Nixon and Kissinger, must always be available to back diplomacy in dealings with Russia. Russia has no respect for weaklings like England and France who were afraid to take a stand for fear of losing Arab oil. America, Holland and Portugal were the only nations to evince the courage, determination and will power to endure sacrifices in backing Israel's self-preservation in her gravest hour of need. It is comforting to the author, who witnessed the destruction of six million Jews while the world stood silent, to see that

---

[20]*The New York Times*, October 29, 1973; *Newsweek*, October 29, 1973.
[21]*The New York Times*, October 29, 1973.

President Nixon and America fulfilled their moral obligation to save Israel by supplying her with a massive airlift of the latest sophisticated weapons in the American arsenal.

Let us analyze the present prospects for peace in the Middle East. Secretary of State Dr. Henry Kissinger was able to work out a compromise agreement for a cease-fire between Israel and Egypt. On Sunday November 11, 1973, for the first time in 25 years, Israeli and Egyptians came face to face to sign a document containing, the following major provisions:

(1) The prompt exchange of prisoners held by Israel and Egypt.

(2) The creation of a United Nations-supervised corridor for provisions for the Egyptian Army's III Corps, which is encircled behind Israeli lines on the eastern bank of the Suez Canal. The corridor would also provide relief for the Egyptian city of Suez. No military supplies would be permitted.

(3) The relaxation of the Arab naval blockade of the strait of Bab-el-Mandeb at the entrance to the Red Sea. All other blockades would be prohibited.

(4) Negotiations between Israeli and Egyptian commanders to adjust the cease-fire line, with no precise line drawn.

(5) Peace negotiations between Egypt and Israel, although not necessarily on a face-to-face basis. Such talks might take place under the auspices of the United States and the Soviet Union, for example. Egypt and Cyprus have been mentioned as possible sites, but the exact timing and site remain to be worked out.[22]

On December 21, 1973 Israel, Jordan and Egypt commenced talks in Geneva under the auspices of the United States, Russia and the Secretary-General of the United Nations. Syria was invited but refused to participate at this time.

There is no question that it is better to talk than to fight. But many questions have to be answered, by Russia in particular, for a genuine cease-fire and peace to take hold in the Middle East. Will Russia continue to encourage the Arabs to fight future battles by supplying them with still more deadly weapons? Who will

---

[22]*The New York Times*, November 9, 1973.

guarantee that in the future there will be no blockade of the Strait of Bab-el-Mandeb, so essential for Israeli trade? How can Russia play her desired role in the Middle East in times of peace since the atheistic philosophy of Communism is so alien to the average pious Arab? There is ample evidence to suggest that the Soviet Union makes her presence felt most effectively by encouraging trouble and fighting in the Middle East. For Russia the ideal situation is the constant friction of no war and no peace. Israel must constantly remind Russia of her power and might so that Soviet leaders will encourage peace and not foment war. Peace must not be imposed by the two mighty powers. Instead, they should attempt to bring the warring parties to the table to achieve the precious jewel in the world, namely, an everlasting peace.

Let us hope that the billions of dollars spent for war will be used in the near future for education, health, and amelioration of the general conditions of the average person in the Middle East. Let us hope that Russia will send technicians to teach about farming rather than soldiers to teach how to kill over 2,000 Israelis. Russia should send consumer technology to the Arabs rather than missiles. It is possible for Arab and Israeli to live in peace and to share their goods and knowledge for the mutual aggrandizement of everyone in the area. To do so the sincerity and goodwill of the superpowers must be assured.

CONCLUSION

Forged in the crucible of Marx's Communist Manifesto, tempered in the fiery furnaces of the pogroms and the repressions of the Tsars, and shaped to tensile strength amidst the degradations and deprecations of Lenin, Stalin, Khrushchev and Brezhnev, the religious and cultural life of Soviet Jewry has endured through centuries of overt and covert discrimination. It is the author's fervent hope that, in the spirit of detente currently being practiced by both the United States and the Soviet Union Russia will forsake these repressive strictures and permanent peace will come to a safe and secure Israel; that Jews will be free to again attain some semblance of religious and cultural creativity in the Soviet Union should they so choose or, if they desire, in their freely-chosen homeland, the State of Israel.

BIBLIOGRAPHY

Agurskii, S. *Di Yiddishe Komisariatn un di Yiddishe Komunitishe Seksies.* Minsk, 1928.

"Alexander III" *Evreiskaia Enciclopedia.* 1906. I, 825-839.

Baron, Salo W. *The Russian Jews: Under Tsars and Soviets.* New York, 1964.

Benjamin, Emil. *Rabbi Israel Salant: Sein Leben and Wirken.* Berlin, 1899.

Berdyaev, Nicolas. *The Origin of Russian Communism.* Ann Arbor, Michigan, 1964.

Berlin, Meir. *Fun Volosin Biz Yerushalayim.* New York, 1933.

Blazar, Isaac. *Or Israel.* Vilno: 1900.

Braude, Simhah Zissel Ziv. *Hokhma U'Musar.* Vol. I. New York, 1957.

—————. *Hokhma U'Musar.* Vol. II. New York, 1964.

Browder, R. and Kerensky, F. (Eds.) *The Russian Provisional Government, 1917.* 3 vols. Standford, 1961.

Bunyan, J. and Fisher, H. H. (Eds.) *The Bolshevik Revolution, 1917-1918: Documents.* Stanford, 1964.

Chamberlain, W. N. *The Russian Revolution, 1917-1921.* 2 vols. New York, 1935.

Chernov, V. *The Great Russian Revolution.* New Haven, Conn. 1936.

Chernyshevsky, N. G. *Selected Philosophical Essays.* Moscow, 1953.

Crankshaw, Edward. *Khrushchev: A Career.* New York, 1966.

Dan, Th. *The Origin of Bolshevism.* London, 1964.

Deutscher, I. (Ed.) *The Age of Permanent Revolution: A Trotsky Anthology.* New York, 1964.

Deutscher, I. *The Prophet Armed: Trotsky, 1879-1921.* New York, 1967.

—————, *Stalin: A Political Biography.* New York, 1969.

—————, *The Prophet Unarmed: Trotsky, 1921-1929.* N.Y. 1959.

—————, *The Non-Jewish Jew and Other Essays,* London, 1968.

Dinaburg, Benzion. *Hibbat Zion.* Vol. I, Tel Aviv, Dvir, 1932.

Dubnow, S. M. *History of the Jews in Russia and Poland.* 3 vols. Philadelphia, 1944.

Dubnow, S. M. *Nationalism and History: Essays on Old and New Judaism.* Edited with an introduction by Koppel S. Pinson. Philadelphia, 1946.

Friedman, Eliezer E. *Sefer Ha-Zichronoth 1858-1926.* Tel Aviv, 1926.

—————. "Toldoth Baalei Ha-Musar" in *Ha-Meliz,* 111, 1897.

Golder, F. A. (Ed.) *Documents of Russian History, 1914-1917.* New York, 1927.

Gordon, Judah Leib. *Kol Shirei Gordon.* Vol. IV. Tel Aviv: 1931.

—————. *Iggerot.* Edited by Isaac Jacob Weisberg. Vols. I-II. Warsaw, 1894.

Ginsburg, Saul M. *Historishe Werk.* 3 Vols. New York, 1937.

Greenberg, Louis. *The Jews in Russia.* New Haven, 1965.

Gurko, V. I. *Features and Figures of the Past. Government and Opinions in the Reign of Nicholas II.* Stanford, 1939.

Herzen, A. I. *My Past and Thoughts.* 6 Vols. Translated by Garnett. New York, 1924-28.

Hecker, Julius F. *Religion and Communism: A Study of Religion and Atheism in Russia.* London, 1933.

Heifetz, Elias. *The Slaughter of the Jews in the Ukraine in 1919.* New York, 1921.

Herzl, Theodor. *Gesammelte Zionistische Werke.* 5 Vols. Berlin, 1934.

—————. *The Jewish State.* Translated by S. D'Avigdor. London, 1934.

Hurwitz, Joseph Yoizel. *Madregat Ha-Adam.* Jerusalem, 1964.

Kagan, Israel Meir. *Ahavath Hesed.* Warsaw, 1888.

—————. *Michtevei Hafets Hayyim.* Edited and an introduction by Ariah Leib Kagan. New York, 1953.

Katz, Dov. *Tenuath Ha-Musar.* 5 Vols. Tel Aviv, 1952-1963.

"The Kishnev Pogrom." *American Jewish Year Book.* 1903-1904. Vol. 5, pp. 19-22, 39, 109, 111-112, 129-130, 133-141.

Kohn, H. (Ed.) *The Mind of Modern Russia: Historical and Political Thought of Russia's Great Age.* New Brunswick, N.J., 1955.

Korey, William. *The Soviet Cage Anti-Semitism In Russia,* New York, 1973.

Lenin, Vladimir. *Selected Works.* 3 vols. Moscow, 1970.

—————. *Sochineniia.* 2nd edition. XXIV (1932), 203.

Lipschitz, Jacob. *Sichron Jacob.* 3 vols. Kaunas, 1930.

Mackintosh, J. *Strategy and Tactics of Soviet Foreign Policy.* New York, 1962.

Malia, Martin. *Alexander Herzen and the Birth of Russian Socialism.* New York, 1961.

Marx, Karl. *Capital: A Critique of Political Economy.* New York, 1906.

Marx, Karl and Friedrich Engels. The *Communist Manifesto. On Religion.* New York, 1967.

Pobedonostsev, Constantine. "The Jews." *Ha-Meliz.* No. 18 (1882).

—————. *Reflections of a Russian Statesman.* London, 1898.

Rosenthal, A. D. *Megillat Ha-Tebah.* 3 vols. Jerusalem, 1929-31.

Schapiro Leonard. *The Communist Party of the Soviet Union.* New York, 1964.

Sakharov, A. D. *Progress, Co-existence and Intellectual Freedom.* Translation and introduction by H. Salsbury. New York, 1968.

Zenziper L. *Eser Shnot Redifot.* Tel Aviv, 1930.

INDEX

Agurskii, Samuel, 31
Alexander II, 8, 79
Alexander III, 9
Alter, Viktor, 49

Baghdad pact, 82 83, 84
Ben-Gurion, David, 74
Ben-Zvi, Isaac, 74
Bessarbets, 13
Bilu, 10
Biro-Bidzhan, 40, 41, 42, 46, 49, 51
Borochov, Ber, 74
Brezhnev, Leonid, 6, 15, 36, 63, 64, 65, 88

Canton System, 8
Catherine the Great, 79
Conscription Law of 1874, 8

Dimanshtain, Simeon, 31, 41
Dreyfus Case, 11
Dubnow, Simon, M., 11
Dubnow's Diaspora Nationalism, 12, 14

Ehrenburg, Ilya, 49
Eliezer ben Yehuda, 12
Engels, Friedrich, 22
Epstein, Mordecai, 20
Erlich, Harry K., 49

Fefer, Itzik, 49
Finkel, Nathan Zvi, 20
Fisanovich, Israel, 48
Frumkin, Maria Y., 34

Gamarnik, Jan, 43
Gaon of Vilna, 16
Ginsberg, Mordecai Aaron, 19
Gordon, A. D., 20
Grodzenski, Hayyim Ozer, 44
Gromyko, Andrei, 81

Haganah, 20
Haskalah, 9, 18, 19, 20
Hegel's Philosophy, 21, 22
Herzl, Theodor, 10, 14
Herzlian Zionism, 10
Hoveve Zion, 10

Israel Baal Shem Tov, 17

Kagan, Israel Meir, 44
Kaganovich, Lazar M., 38, 39, 53
Kamenev, Lev, 38
Khrushchev, Nikita, 6, 36, 43, 53, 54, 55, 56, 58, 59, 61, 77, 82, 83

Khrushevan P. A., 13
Kirov, Sergei M., 43
Kissinger, Henry, 89, 90
Kitchko, Trofim, 59
Kook, Abraham, 20
Kosygin, Alexei N., 63, 68
Kreiser, Jacob, 47

Lebenshon, Abraham Baer, 19
Lenin, Vladimir, 6, 15, 29, 34, 36, 53
Leningrad Trials of 1970, 70
Liberman, Evsei, 63
Lifshitz, Nechama, 66
Litvak, Lily, 48
Litvinov, Maxim, 73

Malenkov, G. M., 82
Malik, Jacob, 88
Manifesto of Communist Party, 22, 23, 26, 27, 92
Marx, Karl, 6, 21, 79
Maskilim, 9
May Laws, 8, 9
Mekhlis, L., 43
Mendler, Gen. Albert, 88
Mikhoels, Solomon, 49
Mir, Yeshiva of, 17
Molotov, Vyacheslav, 46, 84

Nassar, Abdul, 83, 84
NEP, 35
Nicholas I, 8, 79
Nixon, Richard, 89

Pogroms, 13
Phillippe, Louis, 22

Rudin, Elisha, 34

Salanter, Israel, 18
Solzhenitsyn, Alexander, 57
Sharett, Moshe, 84
Sharon, Gen. Ariel, 89
Stalin, Josef, 6, 32, 37, 38, 45, 49, 52 53, 58
Statute of 1835, 7

Tekoah, Yosef, 88
Trotsky, Leon, 37

Versailles, Treaty of 1919, 14
Volozhin, Yeshiva, 17

Yaroslavskii, Emelian, 32
Yevtushenko, Yevgeny, 55

Zinoviev, Gregory, 38

323.119   43887
Ec57s

Eckman, Lester Samuel
Soviet policy towards
Jews and Israel, 1917-
1974.

323.119   43887
Ec57s